RAPE: THE BAIT AND THE TRAP

A balanced, humane, up-to-date analysis of its causes and control

by Jean MacKellar
with the collaboration of Dr. Menachem Amir

Crown Publishers, Inc., New York

Books by Jean MacKellar

HAWAII GOES FISHING
RAPE: THE BAIT AND THE TRAP

Library of Congress Cataloging Publication Data
Mackellar, Jean Scott.
    Rape: the bait and the trap.

    Includes index.
    1. Rape—United States. I. Amir, Menachem, 1930–
joint author. II. Title.
HV6561.M3   364.1'53   75-20311
ISBN 0-517-51877-5

Contents

"The truest sisters are those who work together."

This book is dedicated to the women of the Marin Rape Crisis Center: Ramina, Suzanne, Linda, Trish, Jane, Beth, Jan, Charlsey, Pat, Nita, Diane, Marlane, Betsy.

And to all the women who unite in sisterly support of the victim at the other rape-crisis centers throughout the United States.

Prologue

Dr. Menachem Amir's monumental contribution to the science of criminology was to dismantle, by statistical methods, about a dozen myths on rape that have prevailed for centuries. After his pathbreaking studies, reported in *Patterns in Forcible Rape* in 1971, rape became a respectable topic. The subject moved from sniggering kitchen gossip to thoughtful dinner table talk.

The appearance of Dr. Amir's book coincided with an upsurge in the women's movement. Throughout the country symposiums and meetings were held on women's rights and the injustices of sexism. Rape was one of the major issues. Women who never before had admitted they had been raped spoke out and their voices were bitter and angry. This consciousness-raising tilled the ground so that the seeds of Amir's facts could take on a life of their own in a proliferation of articles in national magazines. Crime rates were rising everywhere across the United States and it became clear that the trauma of rape was a cruel fact among women of all classes and backgrounds, and although more common in some communities than others, a reality in every community. For the first time, men who cared about the fate of women as well as women who cared about their sisters realized that something was seriously wrong, that what had once been police blotter material was in fact material for their own consciences and action.

Once the nation was aroused to the prevalence of the crime, the questions began to be asked: What produces this ugly, gratuitous act? How can it be curbed? Amir's dismantling of rape myths through hard statistical facts proved invaluable in looking for these answers. Myths serve a function. The myths about rape, as we shall see, have served to perpetuate the attitudes that contribute to the crime. The disproving of these myths, then, goes far beyond interest as academic fact; it provides the means for understanding the causes of rape, and hence, for working to reduce it. In this book, the fragments of truth on which the rape myths are based will be examined, as well as the reasons they have survived, with such honor, in our society.

The case histories used to illustrate the errors of the myths usually are not described in their entirety at once, but appear piecemeal, in different contexts, throughout the volume. The outcome of each is resolved in the epilogue, with information about its legal disposition and other facts of interest. Some of these cases are drawn from Dr. Amir's Philadelphia study of 646 victims and 1,292 offenders, some from his interviews with hundreds of other victims in subsequent work on the West Coast. Others are women whom I have known as a victim advocate for the Marin Rape Crisis Center.

Although the work contains harsh criticism about police indifference and insensitivity, based on general reputation in many areas, I'm pleased to report that my personal experience with the police of San Francisco, Oakland, and Marin in dealing with rape victims has been remarkably satisfying. Their service has been far above the traditional, a fact that I attribute in large part to the community education work of women's groups in the Bay Area.

I hope that women will recognize in these pages truths about themselves that help to ease their loneliness in the experience of rape, and I hope that other women, not victims, will see in the victims the evidence of the fragility of their own roles so that they may, in the common risks of sisterhood, become more united.

I wish to express my appreciation to Dr. Amir for his generosity and patience while working with me in this fulfilling project. His faithful correspondence made possible the continuance of our collaboration after he had returned to Israel.

I also wish to thank Richard Graves for his warmhearted help and support in the preparation of this manuscript, and Millen Brand, the editor who believed in me.

Above all, I wish to cite the brave women, unnamed here, who shared their stories with me in this quest for the truth about rape. I hope their experiences will make a little clearer the answer to this curious puzzle: why a woman is victimized in the act she has been taught to esteem above all others.

April, 1975
Novato, California

I

HOW DOES IT HAPPEN: MYTH AND FACT

The Enigma of Rape

"DON'T SCREAM!"

When a woman is seized for rape these are often the first words she hears.

A Berkeley coed hurries toward the English department building to hand in a term paper, due at four o'clock. It is already three thirty; she takes a footpath through the campus grass and trees, a typical University of California figure with long blond hair and comfortable counter-culture clothes—jeans and a brightly colored tunic. A Greek satchel carrying books hangs from her shoulder.

Without warning the girl is seized from behind, a man's hand roughly smothers her face. She is half thrown, half dragged off the path into a stand of high shrubbery. "Don't scream and I won't hurt you," the man's voice warns.

The drama is as old as civilization itself; it has taken place in every locale, been reenacted with women of every circumstance. Only the details change. The Berkeley coed's story varies in its own way.

The girl's arms were pinned behind her; she lay panting with fear and shock. Within moments the man's intentions became clear. She began to plead with him but he showed no concern for her words until she said she couldn't bear the shame of it here; they could go to her room. At that the young man released his grip a little and asked where she lived. It was only a few blocks away, she assured him. He agreed to this, released her, and they stood up. Then the girl made another request. She said she had to turn in her English paper by four—would he permit her to do that first?—it would take only a few minutes. The young man agreed to that also, warning her not to try to run away.

As they walked toward the English department building, the young man said with an air of confidence, "You'll get what you always wanted, it will be really nice." They passed dozens of other students as they entered the building and went to the classroom. The girl handed in her paper without speaking to anyone, her companion watching her closely.

A few minutes later they reached the boarding house where the girl lived. In her room she undressed and submitted to sexual intercourse. When the young man asked her to perform fellatio she refused. Still, he was generally pleased with the encounter and as he left he said, "You're good. I'm good too." He seemed quite at ease as he sauntered away from the boarding house. Slowly the young woman dressed and went to the campus police station.

Was this rape? Has this man committed a crime for which the law should prosecute? The points recited on either side of the argument are not conclusive.

—Yes, it's a crime. The man seized her, she did not in any way provoke the situation.

—She didn't try to extricate herself either.

—The man was a stranger and he forced her.

—He used no weapon, left no marks.

—But he frightened her.

—There was no real violence.

—There might have been. He said ". . . and I *won't* hurt you."

—She had a dozen chances to save herself and didn't.

—That doesn't mean she wanted it. And forced, unwanted sex is rape.

—If she really had not wanted it, she would have resisted.

—She was afraid.

In court the victim would have little chance of obtaining a verdict of guilty against her assailant since there was no evidence of brutality, traditionally required to prove force has been used. The young woman was more than submissive, she was cooperative; she proposed her own room and took him there. The defense attorney would be sure to note that this not only added to the comfort and security of the act, it made it possible for the man to return.

Dr. Amir does not hold that proof of violence is necessary for a case to be bonafide. Although the young woman did not take advantage of chances to extricate herself, she suffered the shock and indignation of the true victim. Her outward behavior failed to conform to expected standards of resistance, but her inner experience was one of victimization. She was not a virgin, says Amir, but she did not want this man, or this act. It was rape.

The place is Honolulu, although the story is so common it could take place anywhere in the United States. Four working women share a cottage. On New Year's Eve one of them arranges a blind date with a navy lieutenant for her roommate, a frail, green-eyed brunette with a shy manner. The evening begins with a party at the Pearl Harbor Officers' Club, goes on to someone's quarters and ends near dawn in the back seat of a Buick. The woman does not like the navy lieutenant. He drinks heavily and has been indifferent to the point of rudeness all evening. Contrary to what he told her, she has found out that he is married. In the car, when he puts his hand inside the bodice of her dress she protests. He only tightens his grip and snarls, "What's the matter with you?" Half an hour later, hardly speaking, they part, never to see each other again. The woman does not know it, but she is pregnant.

She will not report the event; in fact she is so humiliated that she will not even tell her housemates when she learns of her predicament. She will quit her job and leave the Islands.

Hundreds of thousands of cases in which the man and woman know each other go unreported. When the two are not strangers, so many complex elements, legally mitigating for the man, are introduced that the chances are minimal for the woman to prosecute. Not only has this woman failed to defend herself according to the law, but her own sense of moral failure translates into a guilt which would make her a poor witness.

How widespread is rape? There were about 51,000 reported rapes in 1973, an increase of 10 percent over 1972. Most large cities have at least one reported rape per day; New York City had more than 4,000 in 1973. Forty-four percent of all rape in the United States takes place in cities of more than 250,000—one woman out of every thousand in those cities. Statistically, somewhere across the nation a woman is raped each minute of the day.

Although the figures are alarming enough in themselves, the actual facts may be far worse.

If, as is commonly acknowledged, only one out of four sexual attacks by strangers are reported, the estimate for the nonstranger is radically higher. Feminist groups estimate that only one out of ten or perhaps only one out of twenty women tell police about the sex forced upon them by the man whom they met in a bar or who gave them a ride home from a social event.

Besides the victims' personal reasons for not wishing to report, there are other reasons for unrealistically low figures on rape. Women from minority groups have a sense of hopelessness about finding justice within the white man's legal system so they often don't try. Their apathy is justified. Not only are their claims indifferently received but they may not even be processed by law enforcement agencies, which are more concerned with keeping up an efficiency record of "cases solved" than of detailing the troublesome and unresolvable problems of the ghettos.

Of every 100 rapes reported perhaps only 85 will be validated as authentic by the law. Whether a story like that of the Berkeley student would be accepted depends on how enlightened the police force is, and how oriented to women's problems.

Legally, rape is one of the most problematic of all crimes. It is detested in the courts. If a case is not sensational enough to provide a clearcut sense of outrage against the man, then the anger tends to flow back against the woman. The uneasiness associated with confronting other people's sexuality is attached to the victim and her case is tinctured with doubts that are a hangover from a puritanical tradition of purity, virginity, and submission. In no other crime against the person is the victim so likely to suffer a second victimization as when a woman takes the man who has sexually assaulted her to court.

It is the sexuality of the crime which makes for its confusion in men's minds, and in the law, which is a reflection of men's sense of justice. Whole psychological systems have been constructed on man's feelings about his own and women's sexuality. Dealing with these feelings is one of the most delicate, entangled, and threatening of all legal processes. Everyone who is involved in the case, or who follows it, becomes locked into one position or another on what is "fair," depending on the strength of his own sexual ego. All the old myths are retested; everyone's image is at stake. Those whose sexual image is most imperiled take the most vehement position on one side or the other. It is difficult to see the crime as one against the person, like aggravated assault, and to judge it without the blinding, hand-me-down prejudices of former times, other places.

There are still a great many men to whom forcing a woman sexually is not a crime. Resisting sexual advances, they believe, is the normal way for a woman to act, and overcoming this resistance is the way a man is supposed to act. There are many men who have never had it any other way, who indeed may not want it any other way. Rape is still believed by many (including women) to be the just deserts of an overseductive and undercompliant hussy.

As studies of rape continue, two important facts suggest themselves. The first is that the largest problem, the one that is of concern to the most women, is not the most dramatic one—the psychopath who makes a swath in print. Rather, it is the callous violation of a woman's sexual rights by a man whom she knows. As in an iceberg, these events compose the larger, unseen bulk of the problem, while the more sensational cases of rape by a stranger are its visible tip. The fallout from these numerous but less known dramas is only beginning to emerge through the liberating influence of feminist groups, and its role in the havoc of female-male relations is yet to be estimated.

The second fact, of great importance not only in dealing with offenders but in curbing the crime, is that rape is less a sexual attack than one of aggression. Strangers or nonstrangers, the men who force women into sexual relations are generally not motivated by sexual need. Their aggressiveness is a form of exploitation, which, in turn, is an expression of society's general attitude toward exploitable people. The basic attitude of the man who rapes is shared by a large part of his culture.

The idea that rape is due to sexual need is an outgrowth of the self-serving myth of the male's overpowering sexuality, which, besides being bracing to the male ego, has been useful in maintaining a male chauvinist society. Its champions therefore are legion and loud, its roots old and well established.

The myth of the rapist's sexual need has produced equally erroneous corollaries about women. Consider the wicked foolishness in such widely held beliefs as "Women dream of rape, it excites them to be forced." And, "If a woman really didn't want rape she would hold her legs together."

The myths which surround rape have served to obfuscate its real nature. Many of them are now as obsolete as old wives' cures for cancer and nearly as dangerous. Sexuality has entered a new era; the old standards do not apply. Without defending coerced sex in any way, it is only fair to note that the experience of unwanted sex to a woman who has sat through the movie *Deep Throat* is in no way comparable to the experience of our frantically prudish grandmothers, some of whom rarely bathed because they couldn't stand the sight of their own naked body in the tub. Yet most sex laws have not been revised for at least four generations.

Rape is not a single uniform act but a variety of behavior imposed on sexually resisting women. Heretofore all forced sex was wrapped up in the inflammatory word "rape" in which a sexual double standard, obligatory virginity, and a large backlog of free-floating prejudice were implicit. Medieval punishments were considered appropriate. Now it is becoming clear that there are at least three quite different patterns in which women are forced sexually. And that the kinds of men who indulge in rape—or are driven to it—are quite different. The distinctions are important. Much of the error in society's treatment of the crime has come from an inability to make these distinctions. In generalizing about rape both men and women have been disserved.

The old mystique about sexuality must change and surely will. Women are now in a state of flux about themselves, hypersensitive about what they don't want from men, unclear about what they do want for themselves. Some go without bras for ideological reasons, others because it is sexier. Men are beginning to see that the liberation of the woman will bring a new kind of freedom for themselves. What used to be called campaigns for women's rights are now called campaigns for equal rights. In this joyful anarchy of change, which often involves some of the best of human motives, the laws must modify to reflect the new mood.

The case of the Berkeley coed was chosen as an opening illustration of the complexities of rape because it gives the lie to all the old, pat answers: that the offender is a raging sex fiend or that the victim is a provocative hussy who got what she deserved. Or that the offender deserves life (or death, in eleven southern states) or that the victim must be a whore because such things don't happen to "nice" girls.

In the Honolulu story, the navy lieutenant, like most sex offenders, was not a special kind of man, just one who assumed he had the right to impose his desires on a woman who was vulnerable. The personality problems of such a man are not radically different from those of the members in good standing of suburbia's country clubs everywhere. Many men, hearing of the incident, would share this reaction: "The problem is, she got pregnant. That's her fault, because she wasn't on the pill."

The many nuances of this old, troubling, curious, and unjust drama are inherent in these two simple stories of rape by a stranger and rape by a nonstranger: the quirky chauvinism of the male, the appalling passivity of the female. The bait and the trap of the male and female roles in our society. As everyone knows, Bait, no matter how attractive, will go unharmed if there is no Trap; and a Trap will catch nothing if there is no Bait. What produces rape and what might help to reduce it are the concerns of this study. Examining the myths that have helped to perpetuate the grievous old pattern might be a good way to begin.

2

It's Not Sexual Hunger

MYTH: Sexual hunger is the cause of rape.
FACT: Sexual hunger is only one of many causes of rape.

Is it raging lust that drives men to rape? Is the rapist a man tormented by abnormal needs, or deprived of a normal sex life? The more sensational elements of the press have exploited these notions for many years. The truth about why men rape is far more complex. A sex drive is involved in rape; the offender cannot function without it. But many other needs and motives, interlocking and often unconscious, are important in the act of forcing an unwilling woman into a sexual act.

When asked why they raped, many men confess they do not know. This, in fact, is the most common answer, given with a stubborn, baffled air, probably honest. A few men will say, "I needed some cat," or, "Like, it was Saturday night, man." But most seem to have acted without considering the motive. They simply act in response to a feeling.

Ironically, most of them could meet their sexual needs in other, less difficult ways. Sixteen percent are married, about half have more or less regular sexual partners. Consider the case of a big, very good-looking man who admitted he had more women after him than he could handle, yet who waited many hours in the cold and fog to attack nurses at San Francisco's Langley Porter Hospital. When caught after several rapes he was asked why he bothered, since so many opportunities for sex were available to him. He grinned. "Too easy."

On Philadelphia's fashionable Main Line a garbage collector raped nine of his society matron clients in one eight-month period. Why did he do it? The man, a forty-five-year-old black, was full of excuses. His wife, he said, was "old and no good any more" and black women didn't want him. He wasn't paid well enough, he complained, to pay prostitutes, so he raped. His description of the rape events gave a clue to other motives. "I do it in their own bedrooms," he said. "Then I own the house!" Clearly, it was not only the sex that was satisfying but the whole experience.

The garbage collector to the contrary, most blacks can get all the sex they want. Black men are outnumbered by black women, and the subcultural pattern allows for a lot of easy sexual activity. Blacks rarely go to prostitutes; they are proud of the fact that they can get all they need without paying for it. Some black offenders make a point of bragging that their rape was not due to sexual need. "You think I can't get pussy when I want?"

Since blacks account for an overwhelming percentage of reported rape (90 percent) and since they do not rape because of sexual hunger, then clearly another motive is at work. This, it is generally agreed, is rage. The reasons for black male rage in our country are many; the target on which it often focuses is the easiest, a female, usually black.

"There can be a sex crime by an offender whose problem is *sex*," says Amir, "but the fact that so many offenders have a record of violence shows that violence and an attitude of contempt for women are the main problems."

Occasionally men who are just released from prison commit rape. Sexual hunger after months or years without a woman might seem to be reasonable in such cases, but one cannot discount the expression of rage at the society which has locked them up, the hidden desire for revenge the rape reveals.

In one pair-rape, two men who had been released on parole picked up two women and with considerable brutality forced them. In another case, an offender released from prison after ten months for attempted robbery entered the apartment of a single woman by the back stairs, around noon, showing a gun. The woman, who had been washing diapers, was afraid for her baby and submitted without a struggle. "You ain't got a woman, you gotta git it like this?" she asked bitterly. The man said he had been in jail. "I need it in the worst way and I'm gonna git it . . . ."

This crime may have begun as a burglary, although the offender had not taken anything when he was picked up. The act of burglarizing often seems to provoke sexual desire. Many offenders enter a house intending only to steal but stay to rape the woman they find there, if she is alone. This, in effect, is another kind of "penetration."

Typical in some respects was the case of a Jewish woman in Philadelphia. A divorcee in her forties, she was alone in her home, sleeping naked under a sheet on a hot summer night when she was awakened by a burglar who had entered through a rear window. The man asked her where her money was. As she pointed, her breast was exposed. The man came to her bed and forced her to have sex with him. Less common was the way this intelligent woman handled the situation afterward. She talked with the man, asked him questions about himself. He was a young Puerto Rican, terribly thin. He told her he was twenty-seven years old, had been in the United States for five years, was unable to work. He said he had no money, couldn't get a woman. She told him it wasn't nice to rob and rape. He cried.

The confusion of the robber-rapist's motives is illustrated in the case of a seventeen-year-old boy who was in the class with Amir's daughter at a Berkeley high school. Carrying a knife, he entered homes as if to burglarize. He never stole anything, however, only raped the girl or woman he found there. Afterward he would excuse himself to his victim: "I have to leave, someone is waiting for me at home," and depart. When caught, he admitted to thirty-three cases of rape in one month, although the total may have been closer to forty-five. His motive? It seemed that he was on bad terms with his stepfather. Each time they had words the boy would quit the house and rape. Teen-age rebellion? . . . Compulsive rite of passage? . . . An oedipal rage aggravated by the fact that the man was not even his father? . . . The case is a veritable lode of fascinating psychological material. Pretending to the lesser crime of robbery may have been a means of neutralizing his sense of guilt about rape, expressed in the boy's apologetic leave-taking.

The desire to rape may be prompted by a need to prove one's self sexually rather than sexual hunger. Some offenders have confessed to a need to test their image against what they've seen on the TV, to find out if they were "normal," real men. Tall tales among the military ("I have two guns, one is for killing, one is for fun") produce another kind of pressure. One man, desperate to prove himself, had been unable to have normal relations with women because of an extremely small penis. He could not even go to a prostitute; he was too embarrassed. The police had a long record on him for molesting girls. Finally he arranged an operation to have his penis enlarged. When sufficiently healed, what was his unfortunate way of trying out his new, improved resources? Years of an acute inferiority complex cannot easily be wiped out; his old asocial patterns remained. Like many who lack the confidence to win a woman, he raped.

In discussing the sexual nature of rape it is important to note that sexuality in our culture is diffuse and continual. We are surrounded not only by real sexual objects, like braless nymphs, but sexual *symbols*, like sleek, elegant cars. Even before situational stimuli begin there is a latent threshold of response, an inner arousal already prepared. The sexual "field" is never empty, sexual responses never start from zero. Many ordinary acts may be sexually inspired—a decision to swim or go to the races. Sexual motivation is a hidden element in many cases of murder, assault, theft, and arson. Conversely, a sex act can be not just for the sexual relief, but for revenge and other indirect purposes.

Pleasure in destructiveness can be so keen as to acquire a sexual tone. The *Encyclopedia of Murder* reports the bizarre case of a Viennese man who could achieve sexual satisfaction only by arranging and witnessing a train wreck. In 1931 he staged one wreck a month in Amsterdam, Paris, and Marseilles.

Violence and sex, as everyone knows, are all too frequently associated, even *mistaken*. A vast number of people think that violence is sexy and that sex is a sort of battle in bed. This major psychological error has facilitated the explanation that rape is due to sexual need even when the facts so clearly argue otherwise. If a hunger for violence is perceived as the same as a hunger for sex; then *voilà*! How easy to declare that the man who rapes is a sex fiend! The notion provides so many exciting ideas for copy, and besides is more politically acceptable than that of revenge against an exploitative society.

The myth of men's sexual hunger, while finding its most spectacular form in the trauma of rape, is comfortably rooted throughout the broad, sexist base of our culture, useful in many ways. It is responsible for the idea (privately held by such armies of men that one wonders where the "norm" is) "I am oversexed, the way I wake up in the morning proves it."

The notion of being overendowed is pleasant to most men. It elasticizes the self-image, it gives excuse to act out the faintest stirrings of desire. "I can't stand it," they frown, as if manfully hobbling cataclysmic passions. Cataclysmic passions? How many women complain that when they slip into a lacy nightie they find their mate either snoring, out cold, or gasping "I'm dead," from within the pillow. That only when she is safely bathing the baby or preparing a company dinner is he overcome by these passions.

Concomitant with the myth of man's satanic sexual hunger is the well-known corollary, "Women's sexual desire is far weaker than men's." This has a two-pronged usefulness. Since women are thus incapable of understanding men's problem, it restricts valid criticism to the fellowship, which has a lively interest in perpetuating the myth. Secondly, by denying a comparable sexuality in women, by giving them an image of being unneedy, even frigid, men give themselves greater freedom to roam; one woman isn't enough.

The myth of male supersexuality has its historical roots in the biblical nomad's status symbol and visible evidence of virility, his collection of wives. Their number was an index of his prosperity, which in turn depended on the number of useful children the wives bore. His modern descendant is the playboy who dreams of laying a different broad in his sumptuous pad every night. Between the two are several millenia of legends, jokes, and gossip designed to keep the male feeling oatsy and master in the game of sex. If an occasional rape and a general fear of rape help keep women submissive and dependent, ready to exchange sexual favors for defense against the shadowy unknown, who's to bad-mouth a good old myth like that of the infernal "burning"?

Rape among the blind is an unexpected event, the more so when one considers how important visual stimuli are to sexual feelings for the rest of us. How would it be never to have seen a female body, people kissing, glossy hair, a warm smile, colors that make one happy? Amir describes a rape by two blind boys, sixteen years old, of a girl also sixteen, an inmate of the same institution. The rape was planned; the boys knew that after 10 P.M. there was only one matron for the whole building. They waited until they knew she was in another wing, then went to the girl whom they had decided on in advance. When attacked, the girl cried out, arousing others, although they could not understand what was happening or help her. The boys fell over some chairs, adding to the confusion, and the noise soon led to their apprehension.

There was much explorative touching during the event. Without the photos, drawings, and movies which add so much to the experience of the sighted world, the young offenders had no real image of how a woman looks or is formed. Even books with sexual content (such material in braille is not allowed in a home for the blind), which contribute to the free-floating sexuality of our culture, were absent.

The girl was technically a virgin. She had deflowered herself but had no experience with men. This was before courses in sex education were common in the schools; a little hygiene for girls was all that was taught at that time.

The innate sexuality of all human beings is evident in this pathetic attempt to assert maturing needs.

3

It's Not Impulsive

MYTH: Rape is an impulsive act.
FACT: In three fourths of the reported cases rape is planned.

It has been generally believed that the man who rapes acts in a fit of passion with no thought for the consequences. Although offenders may claim they did not know what they were doing, or why, and in fact there are some bizarre instances of this, usually the offender has plenty of time, even days of cool planning, before the attack.

The case of an ex-prisoner, a thirty-five-old white man on parole after serving eighteen months for burglary, is a point in evidence. On his third day out he pushed a young black girl into an empty garage (the location seems to have been prepared), punched her a few times, threatened to kill her, and raped her. Before letting her go he warned her not to report, saying he'd already killed, although this was not true. When interrogated, the man admitted that in prison he had dreamed about how he would rape when he got out. His dream was not about an earth-shaking sexual experience; it was about *rape*.

Amir distinguishes between planned, unplanned, and partially planned rape events. It is also useful to distinguish in each of these categories between the acts of a man who is a total stranger and those of one who is known to his victim.

The planned rape reveals criminal propensities, especially if the victim is unknown. The location, time, and many other factors may be carefully worked out ahead, but the victim may be selected only a moment before the act. When a lone woman is seized on descending at a lonely bus stop, the offender may have planned it a week ahead and waited for hours for the right combination of circumstances. This was the modus operandi of a man who raped seventeen women in different towns of Marin County, finding the early dark evenings of winter propitious for seizing women as they got off the Golden Gate bus, returning from work in San Francisco.

In the planned rape by the nonstranger, an acquaintance or friend may prepare a siegelike seduction, leaning on the knowledge that bars, parties, and holidays are highly charged with sexuality, to help him succeed. If at the critical moment the woman demurs, he forces her with a high-handedness which is the more painful in that it comes as a betrayal of trust. This kind of forced sex is responsible for about half the reported rapes and for many thousands of others never revealed by the stricken victims. A rape is particularly likely to have been planned if it takes place in the home of either the victim or the offender.

A rape can be partly planned: "I want to get laid tonight, I'll go to the Blue Note and find *something*." In such a case the behavior of the woman who is approached may influence whether and how the event is carried off.

An unplanned rape can be put in motion at a drinking party where the atmosphere is eroticized and judgment is blurred; the offender may simply refuse to take "no" from a woman he fancies. This is not an aberrant deafness on his part; years of conditioning have taught him that a woman's "maybe" and "no" can mean "yes" if he puts on enough pressure. Impulsively he pushes her out onto the fire escape, or drags her off into the garden; a shamefaced or angry victim may or may not report it later. This "coerced seduction" is without criminal intent; still it is an antisocial act.

Rape can be an accessory act, an afterthought in a planned crime, as with the young Puerto Rican. For some burglars it is a part of the whole design, just as it is for others to leave a turd in the front hall as their calling card.

The circumstances of a crime situation can provoke an offender to rape, as in the case of the man who tried to rob a grocery store. Wearing a stocking over his face, he entered pointing a gun. Four women were present, the storekeeper and three customers. The man went to the cash register and tried to open it but could not. Furious, he herded the four women into a back room and demanded their money, taking $1 from one, $2 from another, $6 from the third. The utter passivity of his victims in yielding to his demands seems to have been the element in arousing his sexual desire. He opened his pants fly and made each of the four women put her hand on his penis. "Touch it," he said, "it's good." Still encountering no resistance, within the next ten minutes he proceeded to rape one woman standing up, then a second one on the floor, holding his gun to her head. One of the women, who was four months pregnant, he made a point of avoiding.

"I was surprised, myself," he confessed later. "I just got the urge."

There is also the rape that could be described as hastily planned, when a man with the mental set for rape unexpectedly finds himself with the opportunity. Such was the case when a girl who worked as a go-go dancer got off a bus in Oakland and was seized by a man who clearly meant to rape her. She broke away, ran to a nearby parked Volkswagen, and begged the man sitting in it to help her. He got out and chased her assailant away, then kindly told the girl she should return home, have a drink, rest, and try to forget it. He would drive her there himself. When they arrived at her door he pushed his way in and raped her.

When more than one offender is involved in a rape the chances that it is planned leap radically. Whereas 58 percent of the single rapes in Amir's study were planned, 83 percent of the pair-rapes were planned and 90 percent of the group rapes were planned.

Whether or not a rape is planned is an important consideration legally. It helps fix the degree of the offense, just as in homicide the law distinguishes between involuntary manslaughter, murder in the second degree, and coldly calculated murder in the first degree.

Unplanned rapes are often the most bizarre and unaccountable. A flagpole sitter in Texas raped a young girl who was one of his visitors; told her he would throw her off the pole if she didn't yield. The compleat flagpole sitting experience? The ultimate in phallic heights?

One man raped his mother-in-law while his wife was in the hospital having a baby. It was a Sunday; the man had been drunk the night before but was not drinking that morning. He entered the kitchen where his mother-in-law, a large, heavy women of about forty-eight, was drinking coffee, wearing a sweater and bathrobe over her night clothes. Without any preliminaries he seized her and pushed her into the bedroom. The man was both tall and strong, the woman did not resist although she did phone the police immediately afterward. The man expressed no regret when interviewed. "Why'd she have to call the police?" he complained. "I didn't know what I was doing." He may, in fact, still have been foggy from the alcohol of the night before.

In another case a man raped his grandmother. His wife also was pregnant, although several months from delivery at the time. She was not in the house, but the children were playing downstairs when the man approached his grandmother in one of the upstairs bedrooms. She was a lean, trim, well-preserved woman of fifty-eight who smoked a pipe. The family had recently moved to Pennsylvania from the South. The man began to touch the woman playfully; there were some good-natured exchanges, then the tone changed. He began to push and hold her, finally slapped her face and threw her down on the bed. The woman was furious, she reported the event immediately. "After all, he has a wife." The man did not try to justify himself. "I don't know why I did it," he said. Several times during the interrogation the woman blamed the bad morals of the North for the event. "It was the North that did it. This wouldn't have happened in the South."

Rape within families is rarely reported to the police, and black women especially rarely report any rape because they have so little hope of decent treatment within the white man's legal system. Both of these cases involved black families. The fact that the women *did* report shows the degree of outrage they felt at having the taboos of family life violated by men whom they should have been able to trust. The crimes also reveal the degree of male rage latent within these men, a rage that found its focus on those who were closest to them.

Although rape usually begins with a decision made some time in advance, Amir cites one more extreme example of an impulsive event, reconstructed from his interview of the offender, who was caught. A man and his wife, blacks in their thirties, were driving to the movies in Philadelphia one night when the man noticed a girl turning off a busy, lighted street into the quiet, one-way street behind the Franklin Institute, at that hour closed and dark. He stopped the car, told his wife to wait a moment, ran around the corner, and seized the girl. He had to act quickly and was very brutal. He gave her several savage blows, threw her down hard on the pavement in the walkway by the garbage cans. Moments later the man returned to his unsuspecting wife and proceeded to the movies. What produced this rape? The couple had not been quarreling. Although the woman was aware that her husband was not faithful, she accepted it, and their family life with their children was not under any special stress. Again, it seemed to be a case of latent rage, triggered by the sight of a lone female entering a vulnerable situation.

Such impulsive events do occur, they are the dramatic exceptions that supply the basis for the myth. Clearly, it has been useful to perpetuate the notion that rape is impulsive, implying a lack of responsibility for one's acts. Less blame attaches to the offender if he seems to have acted out of passion. The myth of impulsivity and the one of rape as due to sexual need are mutually supporting. *Because* it's sexual it's impulsive. Because men's desires drive them out of their minds, they act on blind impulse.

Not until scrupulous statistical methods were applied to a meaningful sample did the truth out. Because rape is exploitative, because it's built on long-harbored resentments, deep layers of antisocial feelings, it is most often planned: a satisfying scenario thoughtfully composed and fulsomely rehearsed in the mind of the offender before he begins to carry it out.

Sometimes the offender studies a selected female for days, as in the case of the San Francisco eighteen-year-old with the frightful modus operandi of trying to incinerate his victims. In the last rape before he was caught, he entered an apartment by breaking a window, tied up the woman, forced her to commit fellatio, poured wine over her body, beat her badly, then set fire to the bed. The woman was found unconscious, with second- and third-degree burns. The young offender had followed the woman, although she was unaware of it, for two weeks before the crime.

When murder follows rape it is usually an accident, either an excess of brutal fury or a postcoital panic. When it is planned, usually the protagonists know each other, and are caught in an inextricable emotional web in which death seems the only solution to the desperate man. A jilted lover or estranged husband will occasionally, in a last parody of their former lovemaking, force a woman into intercourse, then kill her. Although spectacular journalistically, the list is short.

For a man to contrive the rape murder of an unknown woman, planning it from the attack through the sexual achievement to murder and the palpable evidence of a lifeless body, shows a psychopathic turn of mind. William Heirens, the famous rapist who knew he would kill, wrote his plea in lipstick beside the corpse of a victim: "Catch me before I kill again."

4

It's Not the Victim's Sex Appeal

MYTH: It is the irresistibility of the victim that produces rape.
FACT: It is the vulnerability of the victim that produces rape.

On a warm spring evening two women pass each other in San Francisco's animated North Shore district. One is young, with long hair; her skintight bell-bottoms clearly have been chosen for the rearview effects they achieve. The other is a middle-aged woman in the widow's weeds of the Old Country. She carries a bag of groceries which seems heavy for her. The girl buys a pizza, meets some friends, drives away with them. The widow trudges through the nearly empty streets of her modest neighborhood past a block of apartments under construction, quiet since the departure of the workmen.

An hour later a hysterical account of rape is being poured forth in the local police station. But it is not the girl in the skintight bell-bottoms whose clothes are ripped and powdered with cement dust, whose face is swelling under already apparent bruises. It is the widow.

One of the most pervasive myths about rape is that the offender is driven to the deed by the attractiveness of his victim. "Ravished by her beauty," he was compelled to ravish her.

The fact is, the desire to rape does not depend on the desirability of the woman. Although sexual in its mode, the crime is one of violence and aggression rather than eroticism. The man who rapes is attracted by the defenselessness of the victim, not her face or body. Nothing in the dress, physique, or manner of the widow invited sexual attention. But her isolation and frailness invited aggression. She was raped because she was vulnerable. It is not the real beauties who are the most often raped. Many victims are women whom the offender would not date if he could. Statistically, Miss Universe has less chance of being raped than an aging waitress in an all-night greasy spoon. The widow was attacked because, in the famed words of the mountain climber, she was *there*.

The old, the very young, the weak, the isolated and unprotected—these are the easy prey of the offender. The number of mental and retarded patients in institutions who are raped by the attendants remains among the hidden statistics. In Amir's Philadelphia study of 646 rape cases, 51 victims were under the age of ten. There were 123 girls between the ages ten and fourteen; more than a quarter of the victims had not yet reached their fourteenth birthday.

If sexual attractiveness were the basis for rape, the provocative women's clothes of today—miniskirts, see-through blouses and crotch-high cut-offs—should produce whole new waves of crime. Although rape has continued to rise steadily in the past decade, its connection with the new permissiveness in dress has not been proved. Sexy clothes may contribute to more relaxed patterns of sexual behavior, but more and easier sex has nothing to do with sexual assault. Nor has any connection been established between rape and the new proliferation of erotic books and movies. In his experience with more than 2,000 cases, Amir has never interviewed an offender who said he raped because he was stirred by a movie, a book, or what a woman wore.

Reversing the postulate may make a point. If sexual stimuli were to lead in an automatic chain reaction to unbridled sexual desire and hence to sexual assault, mayhem would prevail in our culture. We would have sex riots around the porno book shops, group rapes when half the movies let out, and thousands of sexual attacks, each summer, all day long, on the beaches. In West Germany, where ham is advertised by posters of pigs copulating, there is no evidence that this "progress" in explicitness produces any more rape. Or any less, either.

The fact is that although sexual stimuli are seeded through every aspect of our lives today, reactions to them generally range from unseeing indifference to mild, private lusts that go no further than a few nods and jokes. There are two important missing links between feeling sexual desire and passing to a sexual attack. One is an appetite for power that feeds on exploiting the weak. The other is an attitude of patronizing contempt for women.

While the expression of this contempt is concentrated in the person of the one female in each rape, the feeling is a generalized one: it is as satisfied with one victim as another, and finds its focus on the woman who appears unable to defend herself.

Necrophilia is a form of rape. Though not a common one, and certainly psychotic, it is a pathetic acting out of virility on the most unresisting of all victims, a female corpse. There are men who exhume graves for this purpose. "I can do anything I want with them," said one necrophile who was found digging up a grave soon after the departure of the family. "They don't frighten me."

One-eyed Charley, who became the terror of the Oakland area in 1970, was typical of the rapist's catholic taste in victims. He worked out of parking lots, about twilight on Thursdays, when stores are open until 9 P.M. "I love women," he confessed, when he was apprehended. "Any women. It's not hard to get them, you know. I get them." No woman was safe from him, no matter what her age or condition. Before he was caught, he raped twelve women, eight white, four black. One of his victims was sixty-eight years old, another was eight months pregnant. To be accurate, it should be added that there was one kind of female he did not molest: teenagers. They frightened him.

Sexual attractiveness plays a role in one kind of rape, the failed seduction. In parties and other gatherings where the situation may be eroticized, men provide and women respond to attentions and flattery that carry sexual overtones. The precarious game of the coquette and the gallant is an old and socially honored one. The fine line between it and more serious intentions can be misinterpreted. With the male ego at stake and a mentality that assumes that women need to have their minds made up for them, the game may turn ugly, particularly if the man has been drinking. Male-female relations, being dependent on assumed inhibitions and understandings, are loaded, and it is the female at whom the gun is always pointed.

The element, then, that tempts an offender to rape has nothing to do with the victim's beauty or personal charm. The trigger in the situation is the man's conviction that he can succeed. Where he does not feel he can succeed there is no interest. The décolleté of Elizabeth Taylor, scenes of nymphs rolling around in porno flics do not arouse him.

But that old lady news vendor who will soon lock up her stand and walk to the now-deserted subway entrance . . .

5

It's Fear, Not Brutality

MYTH: In rape the victim is subdued by brutality.
FACT: In most cases the rape victim is subdued by fear.

By definition rape is an act of brutality. The word comes from the Latin *rapere*, which means "to take by force."

Traditionally courts have demanded evidence of brutality to be sure that a case of rape is authentic. Criminologists and women's liberation groups quarrel with the law. They insist on taking into account fear of brutality, which can be just as effective. A girl with a knife at her throat may escape without a mark on her, yet the threat is more serious than a few blows, which she might try to match.

Classically, the offender threatens to strangle, beat, or stab his victim if she resists, while promising no harm if she complies. "Don't make noise, don't fight, and I won't hurt you." In a choice like this, not resisting is only good sense. In this way, the offender is able to eliminate the physical evidence that rape was committed. However brutality can occur and its dimensions can be horrifying.

Amir was the first criminologist to classify the amount and kind of violence used in rape, which ranges from half-playful holding and refusing to release in coerced seduction to outright murder. He expands the term "brutality" to include nonphysical forms such as verbal coercion. Like heavy profanity that sticks. Or threats of harm: "If you don't want anything to happen to your job . . ." (or "your little sister"). Intimidation: "I was a Marine, do you know what I can do with these hands?" (threatening gestures or showing a knife). Intimidation with a weapon: "You scream and you'll have four inches of this blade in your gut," (the threat reinforced by the weapon).

These last two more aggressive forms occur in two thirds of the cases where nonphysical force is used. They are especially prevalent when black rapes black. Blacks are more accustomed to heavy profanity than whites.

Physical force is classified by degrees of violence. Roughness: holding and pushing around. Nonbrutal beating such as slapping. Brutal, which includes beating, choking, and gagging.

Few women are physically brutalized during rape. In 87 percent of Amir's cases the woman was subdued verbally, by fear. When brutality does occur, it is usually before the event, to control the victim and get her to a secure place. Often it is no more than a few blows to show he means business.

Occasionally there is some violence during intercourse. An offender can become very brutal if, after he has achieved penetration, the victim wrenches away. He may beat her face severely. "Men in a fit of rage or sexually frustrated," says Amir, "are capable of anything. They are ugly."

Occasionally an offender will bite the nipple off a girl's breast in one savage snap. Amir had several victims who were in the hospital from this. The men were not psychopathic sadists, just in a rage.

One or two percent of the victims are damaged genitally. Only a really sick man will claw at a woman's organs or resort to poking her with an instrument like a bottle or stick. Aberrant rapists have also stuffed women with twigs and leaves, and one maniac tried to push a shoe up a woman's vagina.

Some offenders become brutal if the victim doesn't cooperate in what he tries to pretend is "lovemaking," to avoid the onus of rape. He asks her to raise her thighs, to move her hips; if she refuses he hits her.

Does an offender ever beat his victim in order to get more reaction and more resistance from her? A man who is gratified by the conquest rather than the sexual act may find additional pleasure in provoking her to struggle, which will justify more physical and sexual brutality. Generally the violence is practical in nature, to subdue the victim.

The worst violence in rape occurs in two distinct situations: group rapes and rapes that take place out of doors. In group rape less violence is actually needed, the intimidation of their number being sufficient to subdue the victim, but the offenders' show of masculinity is at stake. In rapes that take place out of doors the offender must not only reduce the victim to compliancy, but must keep her quiet while moving to a safe place for the act, if he has seized her in a public place like a bus stop.

According to statistics, black men are rougher with their victims than whites. They beat and choke women with more brutality; whether the victim is black or white does not matter.

After intercourse an offender may beat his victim again if he is dissatisfied with the sexual act. If he is of a particularly sadistic inclination he may beat her just for the pleasure of it, or to work himself up to a sexual pitch so he can rape again. Not all rapes end, like that of the Berkeley student, with one sexual act. In 43 percent of the cases in Amir's study the offender subjected the victim to repeated sexual intercourse. This was especially true among black offenders.

The worst brutality may come at the end of the event, when the man wants to convince the victim that she should not tell the police, or when a panic seizes him. After his passion has cooled and he sees the enormity of what he has done, he may try to eliminate the evidence of the fact by doing away with the victim. When a girl's body is found with twenty-six stab wounds, this is what has happened. The offender has gone berserk and acted in a state of temporary insanity.

However, most men apply only such abuse as they feel is necessary to convince the woman that she should not go to the police. When the offender feels reasonably assured of her cooperation he will let her go without further trouble.

Amir includes what he calls "sexual humiliation" in his study on brutality. This is oral sex, both fellatio and cunnilingus. Voyeurism is also a form of humiliation, found chiefly in gang rapes. Fellatio is sometimes used by men who have difficulty in getting or sustaining an erection. Also, it is often demanded by black men of white victims. Symbolically, the act is one of forcing the woman into abject subservience, which may have satisfying racial overtones.

Many victims find it difficult to talk about this element of the event. They don't know the word "fellatio" and are ashamed to describe it, so the attack may be underreported. For a sexually inexperienced girl this part of the act is one of its most traumatic elements. A young victim may never have seen a man's penis in erection, may hardly be aware of her own sexual organs. To be forced to put her mouth on a phallus may produce such a shock of revulsion that she becomes ill. She may have vomiting attacks for days afterwards.

In one third of Amir's cases fellatio was included. In 6 percent cunnilingus was used. Cunnilingus takes time and a sense of security; it is usually practiced indoors or in a car. In 6 percent of the cases both forms were involved. These activities are more common among whites than blacks. In group rape, which is a form of sexual humiliation in itself, fellatio and cunnilingus are common and seem to be a part of the testing of roles that members feel obliged to play.

Does a show of fear on the part of the victim invite further brutality? Amir's answer is both yes and no. A few men enjoy inflicting pain, are stimulated by the sense of power that comes with terrifying a victim. Most brutality stems from the fact that the man is stronger than the woman, and her resistance obliges him to use his strength. "They give you trouble," some men complain. "If they didn't fight it would be better for both of us."

Is it useful for a woman to try to talk her way out of the situation? No. If a girl says she's menstruating she may be forced into sodomy. Saying that she's pregnant does no good at all, and the appeal to a better nature—"I'm a mother"—goes unheard. "I'm in love with somebody," one girl said. "How could I bear it?"

"You can always say you had no choice," was the grim answer.

Occasionally an offender will show some consideration for his victim. Once in a while, in a gentlemanly move, one will spread his coat on the ground or floor for the girl to lie on. Or her panties. If they are outside the man usually does not take off his clothes though he will indoors or in a car. In a few cases the offender has asked the woman to undress him. More typical is the command "Take off your pants." Some men bring their own condoms, which Amir finds more humiliating than cunnilingus, "The guy is raping her, but he doesn't want *her* to give *him* any problems." In Berkeley, one man asked the girl if she was on the pill. There was one case of coitus interruptus, to protect the girl from pregnancy. One man put his hand under the girl's head and said "Hold me, pretend you're my girl."

How cruel, how pitiless can rape be? In one case a man and his wife captured and tied down a young girl. The man raped her and then had his dog use her. The woman did not touch the girl herself, although she voyeuristically looked on.

In one famous psychopathic case reported by De River, a man killed a very old woman, then raped her and cut off pieces of her flesh, which he ate.

One of Amir's victims received such a severe beating that she died. The woman was sixty-eight years old but in good health before the attack. She was awakened in her home in a pleasant suburb of Philadelphia by a burglar with a black mask over his face. He asked where her money was; she was so terrified she was unable to speak. Furious, the man beat her brutally on the face and body. Then he tore off her pajamas, beat her again, and raped her. She fought, he choked her. After he left she staggered to the next apartment and fainted. She was taken to the hospital in a coma and lived only three days. Amir interviewed her with an attorney because a witness from the justice department, not law enforcement, is needed in court to give the testimony of a victim who is deceased, and they knew she would die. Her vital organs were battered beyond repair. The woman knew she was dying. Although her trachea was so badly damaged she had difficulty in talking, she cooperated with the men, describing the event.

The girl who was raped by the man on his way to the movies was another case of bad brutality. Her face was badly beaten, her jaw broken. Amir interviewed her in the hospital. There were bruise marks on her body from the man's fists, her face was swollen; her head had been banged on the pavement. When she fell on the sidewalk she injured her elbow, an injury known to cause an especially severe pain that diminishes the ability to fight back. The whole encounter lasted between seven and ten minutes. Virgins have more bleeding and pain than sexually experienced women and this girl was a virgin.

There are many more rape attempts than there are rapes. If a door slams in a neighbor's apartment, if footsteps are heard, or a car approaches, a frightened offender may jump up, even if he is already on top of his victim, and flee. Between terrorizing the woman and panicking himself, a rapist may exhibit a wide range of human behavior.

"It's human beings that rape," says Amir. "In every case there's always the human element."

6

It's Often Not the Stranger

MYTH: The man who rapes is a stranger.
FACT: More often than not, the man who rapes and his victim know each other.

For generations the belief has persisted that rape is a crime committed by a vile stranger who lurks in the shadows, waiting for a luckless female passerby. It is the companion to the myth that the man who rapes is one who is in dire sexual need.

The uses of the stranger-rapist myth are many. Not only does it keep women off the streets and contained in their homes in chaste activities, it makes them dependent on the gallantry of men they know, as escorts, if they want to leave their homes. And it also removes their defenses against the sexual advances of these protectors, since, inversely, *their* aggressiveness could not be rape.

The passivity of women is thus arranged to keep them not only chaste and dependent but also vulnerable to men on the inside track. This psychological vulnerability is reinforced by a legal vulnerability, for while there is ready public sympathy for the victim of an attack by a stranger, it is almost impossible for a woman to explain to a court how a friend or acquaintance has undergone an apparently Jekyll and Hyde transformation into a rapist. Even in her own circles the victim's story is often met with heavily skeptical interpretations.

Yet police records show that more than half the victims who report rape know their offenders. If the number of rapes that are reported to police is only one out of three, or as some estimate, one out of ten, then a large percentage of the unreported rapes are likely to be by offenders known to the victims, since there is less to deter a victim raped by a complete stranger from reporting. This would raise the total of known offenders enormously, perhaps to 80 or 90 percent of all rapes.

In the Philadelphia study only 42 percent of the offenders were complete strangers to their victims. Among the 58 percent who were not unknown, Amir analyzed six degrees of familiarity. The least known, a man with whom the victim had had no previous contact although she had some knowledge of him, accounts for 10 percent of the cases. Acquaintances made up 14.4 percent of the cases, close neighbors 19.3 percent, a close friend or boyfriend 6 percent, a family friend 5 percent, and a relative 2.5 percent. Thus, in 33 percent, in the last four categories, the offenders were not only known to the victim, but known well, and were in relationships in which one would normally assume trust.

How can it be that men who seem to be normal, friendly, apparently responsible personalities are transformed into heartless violators of a woman's sexual integrity and breakers of the law? Are they a special breed, a singular type, masquerading behind smiles and everyday activities, waiting for a change in a phase of the moon to become a preying monster? Or is it the woman's fault? Does she bewitch him into this transformation? How is it she suddenly finds herself the victim of someone she has trusted? Is she provocative? Insensitive to signals? Not very bright?

Part of the explanation lies in the psychology of the aggressive role assigned to males in their relations with females in our society. An even larger part lies in the role assigned to the female. One of the (many) burdens that society has laid on the female is responsibility for the social graces. She is supposed to be sweet-faced, chatty, good-hearted; it is up to her to keep the social machinery oiled with smiles and small talk. A man may be surly, gruff, or churlish, but such words could never conceivably be applied to one who is truly feminine. Trained from early childhood, by rewards and punishments, to the manners expected of "a nice little girl," females grow up in a tradition that deprives them of the same rights to privacy and honest feelings as are granted to males. (Compare the macho scowls of the male models in magazine advertisements with the simpering acquiescence on the faces of the females.) Men can smell bad, say unforgivable things, break all the social rules; it does not make them less manly to do so; as the antithesis of femininity, it may even make them more manly. But it is an understood dictum of the womanly graces that a female should make herself into an image pleasing to men. Women who fail to try to please are seriously penalized, because such a failure represents a threat to society. If women should abandon the role assigned to them, it would throw out of shape the whole structure on which male privilege is based. Male privilege is built on the image of woman as a personality arranged to please the man. Thus, to esteem herself as feminine and pleasing, a woman must respond amiably to men when they show themselves disposed to be friendly with her.

There is one other factor at work, which has been described by Gloria Steinem as the "man-junkie" syndrome. Women, she says, have been made to feel that without men they have no identity. They have become as dependent on men as a junkie on his fix, for a sense of well-being. When a man is aggressively friendly with a woman, her first reaction is one of pleasure. She is flattered; his attention fits with her image of herself as society wishes her to be. Unless he becomes an outright boor—physically aggressive—she is likely to interpret his behavior with a maximum leeway of grace, as part of the delightful ritual of testing the potential of a courtship situation. Why should she cut short what is for her one of the most satisfying of all phases of a relationship with a man? His masculine attentions bring out the feminine qualities she has been taught to approve most in herself.

In playing the part for which she has been groomed, she is at her most vulnerable. The truth is, she is not so much provocative as responsive—responsive to the flattery of interest, responsive to the role she has learned. In so reacting, she often fails to heed signals which would warn her that the man's understanding of the ritual may not be the same as hers, and that he may not agree to let her dictate the rules and limits.

Consider the following scenario, which for simplicity's sake takes place between two strangers, although it applies, in the psychology of its escalation, to relations between acquaintances and friends as well:

The setting is public, the man asks the woman a question—Where is the library? Is the bus late? Can I be of assistance? A polite answer is required and this opens the door to some friendly conversation, which, unless she is a "cold, neurotic, ball-busting bitch and probably a dyke to boot," she cannot suitably refuse. Once the dialogue is established, then the man is no longer a stranger. If he suggests having a drink, escorting her to her destination, or strolling in the park, and she refuses, then she is cynical and *unkind*. For although strangers can be dangerous, this man is clearly being friendly, and friendliness is quite the opposite of what is to be feared from strangers. If she continues to play her role as a sociable and acquiescent female and agrees to one of his offers and the man becomes sexually aggressive, it is then *unfair* to reject him because she is switching signals. She has encouraged him until then, hasn't she? The little tramp should be punished for teasing. And he knows just what she deserves, after leading him on like this.

The same pattern is at work when the two already know each other because they are working colleagues or members of the same neighborhood or social circles, the male manipulating and the female permitting advances in familiarity. The myth of the rapist as a stranger completes the geometry of the trap set by society for the conforming female.

Given: the docile role of the pleasing woman.

And: the aggressive rights of the macho man.

But: according to the myth, only strangers rape.

Therefore: what's happening can't be rape.

Conclusion: she is only an idiotic female who doesn't know what she wants and is having her mind made up for her, and what jury will convict for that?

The female succumbs, apparently to male pressures, but in fact she has capitulated, inch by inch, because of her own built-in judgment against herself and fear of being found "unfeminine," "unlovable," "a failure as a woman." For although a man is judged by his *productive* role, a woman is always judged by her *sexual* role. It is always her personality as a sexual being that is on trial. Of course, in failing to maintain her sexual integrity she is also a failure, so she is damned if she does and damned if she doesn't. A more complete trap could hardly be devised.

Concomitant with the myth that the rapist is a stranger, with its corollary that you have nothing to fear from those you know, is the idea that if you get to know someone, then you no longer have anything to fear from him. It is responsible for the kind of innocence that led a music teacher to assume that nothing but arpeggios were going through the head of her new pupil as they sat at the piano in the big, unlockable old mansion that she shared with four other people, all absent during the day. When the young man answered her ad in the local paper she had welcomed him as a pleasant change from the untalented old ladies and restless children who were her usual pupils. The first lesson was mannerly and serious; on their second meeting she was raped. "How could he?" she asked later. "He'd told me all about himself."

Looking back at what happened, the victim often sees clearly moments at which she could have acted to change the course of the event, and this makes her feel guilty and foolish. Her sense of humiliation and outrage at the violation of her trust (and subconsciously, at the trap in which playing her role has placed her) puts her into an almost irreconcilable conflict with her sense of self-respect. For it is not just the most private part of her physical being, her sexual organs, that has been violated but her *sexuality*, the very fountainhead of her personality. How can she ever be the same again?

Until the women's liberation movement raised the level of women's consciousness of their own rights, many women buried such events in their memories, tried to pretend that they never took place. At a symposium on rape, one woman, her voice low and bitter, related her case of several years earlier. "I thought I'd been unfairly had," she said, "but it never occurred to me to tell anyone, or to think of it as rape. I was so hurt then, and so ashamed. But now," she said, her voice rising, "I understand what happened—I see what that bastard did—and I'm mad!"

There is still so little credulity and sympathy for the victim of the known offender that some district attorney's offices refuse to take such a case. "It would be a waste of the state's time," said one deputy. "No jury would convict, so why try?" Such was the reaction to the complaint of a young book editor who was pair-raped by the man with whom she had earlier had a brief, unsatisfactory love affair, and his buddy. Six months after the affair was over the two men arrived at her apartment at midnight and pushed their way in. Her ex-lover hit her repeatedly in the face, slammed her against the refrigerator so hard that she broke three hair curlers and passed out briefly. For three hours they drank and took turns raping her. They were caught on the premises by the police, in full evidence of their brutality, but the woman was considered too compromised to prosecute. The case was dropped.

It seems worthwhile to distinguish between *there are* two kinds of offenders who are not complete strangers to their victims, because the frequently just charges of irresponsibility made for the one are too often applied in sweeping, emotional generalizations to the other. There is the offender whose contact or relationship with the victim has begun in a different context from the one leading to the rape (work associate, friend of a friend, and so forth). And there is the offender who becomes slightly known to his victim through the situation that precipitates the rape, and that is initiated by her. Entering a bar alone would be such a case, so would hitchhiking. (A bar is traditionally male territory, and so is the road; the usual rules do not apply and any female who puts herself in this territory where male definitions prevail is under a double burden to make her own definitions stick.) In entering such situations, where trouble is an obvious, built-in factor, women often act with appallingly naive

follows

hopefulness. The rape that is a sequel to such defiantly imprudent acts should be distinguished both from the stranger rape and the rape by an offender who has known the victim in another context. The blame of irresponsibility in the one case should not be allowed to muddy judgments about the other, as they are quite different.

The most traumatic rape, and probably the least reported of all, is that which involves relatives. In Amir's study, the 2.5 percent in this category of offenders were cousins, uncles, and, most often, relatives by marriage. Father-daughter incest was not included although it is estimated that incestuous acts have been committed in two million families in the United States. Information on this subject is becoming increasingly available from psychotherapists and from women's sensitization groups. Brother-sister rape is also being admitted with more frequency, although these cases rarely if ever reach the police.

Intimate living situations of any kind provide stresses of a sexual nature, and the small, nuclear homes of our epoch are particularly charged with tensions, all the love-hate energy of both sexes being centered on the two parents instead of being spread through the alternative male-female images provided in more extended, multigenerational families. The limited number of bedrooms in the apartments and small homes of today often requires, when friends or relatives are visiting in the home, a doubling-up in the sleeping arrangements. No assumptions can be made; it is a wise parent who prudently foresees problems that the young adolescents may not yet be conscious of.

A new family circumstance, and one that is appearing with greater frequency as more and more marriages are dissolved by divorce, is the formation of new households with offspring from previous relationships. This is a delicate situation when the children, with their confused ties and complicated emotional needs, are only tots and grade-schoolers. When they are teen-age girls, maturing under the same roof with a man who is of no relation to them, and perhaps new in the house too, the situation is indeed volatile. The Electra impulse—the highly charged attraction between daughter and father—is always latent and the original taboo is not present against the allure of this male head of the household who is not the real father. The ripening child-woman, unsure of her sexuality, unclear about her relationship with this potent male figure in the house, unclear, in fact, about nearly everything except a yen to try out the new feminine role that goes with her budding breasts and new pubic hair, may indeed act in disturbing and provocative ways. Responsible males may be outraged to find these young nymphs foraging in the fridge in see-through underwear, or diving for the shower clad only in a charm bracelet. At this moment the little temptress needs wise and firm guidance by her mother. A clever and loving woman, understanding the origin of these family tensions, can forestall regrettable scenes.

Unfortunately, not all women possess either the insight or the affectionate patience to weather such crises. Amir found that in cases of rape between the real father and his daughter, the mother often played an important complicit role. Classically, the mother despises the father, who is of a weak character and frequently a heavy drinker. She treats him with contempt and denies him sexual relations. The enraged man, unable to vent his anger on his wife, takes it out on his daughter, who, as she matures, senses a sexual threat and may even appeal to her mother for help. The uncaring woman, however, in moves designed to humiliate the man further, ignores her daughter's cry for protection and consciously or unconsciously provides opportunities for a crisis by leaving them alone together, where the girl is defenseless.

This psychological pattern has been established many times in incest histories, yet for all her guilt in sacrificing her daughter, the mother is not legally responsible for her diabolical part in the triangle. Where the mother is a strong and protective figure, the daughter is unlikely to be harmed.

Although rape by the known offender is probably more commonplace, the attacking stranger also does exist; he is not a myth. Every day, across the country, dozens of women are seized, especially on the street and after the twilight hour, if they are alone and vulnerable. However, they may also be attacked by strangers in their own homes, and in the daylight hours. A librarian was roused at seven in the morning by a man asking to use her phone because there had been an automobile accident nearby. There had been no accident; when she admitted him to her apartment, he tied her hands and feet with her stockings and raped her.

In the Philadelphia study, 12 percent of the rapes were committed in the victim's home by a man she had never seen before. Black women, it was found, are more likely to be raped by a close neighbor, white women by an acquaintance, but the percentage of rapes by strangers for both races was about the same. Most of the interracial rape was by strangers.

Robbery is the principle crime committed against strangers. If the victim is a woman and the location secure enough, then why not rape too? Then it's a "bank night" for the offender. The rape is a lucky extra which, even if he is caught, may go unpunished, for in plea bargaining the offender gets off on the least serious count. However, this is rarely a consideration for offenders, who act without regard for consequences.

Robbery may have been the original motive in one of the more bizarre cases in Hawaiian crime, the attack of a sailor on the mother of a bride-to-be. The event took place in one of Waikiki's largest hotels, where the parents had come for their daughter's wedding. The sailor tracked the matron through the hotel corridors, raped her in one of the rooms.

The rape of the librarian may also have begun as an attempted burglary; one of the offender's first moves was to ask for her purse, although he showed no interest when she told him where to find it. When an offender plans a rape, the taboo of a sexual penetration may be too strong for him to admit even to himself that this is actually what he seeks. He provides himself with the excuse of a lesser crime, robbery or burglary. It is hard to say, "I want to rape a woman," yet once he accosts a victim, her fear and her fleshly presence can produce in him a sense of excitement accompanied by a rare thrill of power. He may find himself capable of acts of which he had not so much planned as dreamed, even unusual physical feats, such as several ejaculations in a very short time.

It is clear that how little or how well the victim knows the man has no bearing on whether or not he will rape her. There are cases of every degree of familiarity: the man driving to the movies whose decision was made in a split second when he saw a girl turn down a rarely frequented street; the widow who recognized her assailant as someone with whom she had crossed paths in the neighborhood; the music teacher who had given one lesson to her new pupil; the book editor who had had a love affair six months earlier with the offender.

The greatest threat, statistically, to the female's sexual integrity is not the predatory stranger but the aggressive friend or acquaintance. And in this regard, the real peril to the woman is not the man's physical violence so much as her own mental set, in which the fraudulent hopes and prizes implanted by a patriarchal system of privilege weaken her to a vulnerability interpreted as "readiness to consent."

7

It's Not Always Hasty

MYTH: Rape is a hasty, nonverbal event.
FACT: Rape often includes much talk and is prolonged over several hours.

The idea that rape is a hasty event is the logical adjunct of the idea of the surprise attack by the stranger. In the cinema of rape that plays in most people's heads, the man captures his prey and with perhaps no more than a leer (proof that he is a sex fiend) and a few contemptuous blows (for of course the victim would not submit except to overwhelming brutality) he ravishes her and abandons her, defiled in body and broken in spirit, a few minutes later.

The fact is that since more than half of the reported rapes are by friends and acquaintances of the victim, the complex of interchanges that produces rape often takes many hours. The event is not a single sexual act of straight copulation but a series of maneuvers, sexual and otherwise, in which there is frequently a lot of talk, and a relationship of a curious nature develops between the two participants. This can also be true when the offender is a total stranger. While the relationship could never be described as one of friendship, and certainly not one of confidence or trust, there is still room for a spectrum of wide feelings on the part of the victim, besides the dominant ones of fear and helplessness.

One of the most common is *disbelief.* In spite of what she sees and feels, the victim often cannot really believe what is happening. If the man is someone she knows, often she frantically searches for some key to reverse the situation, to turn it back to where it was before. Confused, even stunned, to find a superfriendly being transformed suddenly into an angry and brutal one who must have his way, sexually, at any cost, she may be reduced to a variety of childishly impotent behavior. She may argue, beg, or weep, seek his pity, as if he were the rational person she had first taken him to be. She may try to bargain with him, offer him money, a ring, promises of future friendship and esteem if only he will let her go. Such theatre may serve to amuse her assailant, to enhance his sense of power and prolong the "high" he finds in her subjugation to his will, or he may feel threatened by it, become annoyed and impatient. To stop the verbalizing, in which women often have great resources, he may curtly tell her to shut up, or he may resort to violence.

Another common reaction from women who are too blocked in their feelings to experience their real pain and anger is, incredibly, *embarrassment.* It is a sorry commentary on what society has done in its oversocializing of the female conscience that women frequently refrain from screaming or running to people nearby for help, not out of fear of what their assailant may do, but because they do not want to *bother* others, or to call attention to the despicable position in which they find themselves. Such has been her training that "nice girls" don't make rude noises or press untoward demands on others that a victim often prefers to hide her disgrace and to struggle through her plight alone, at whatever cost to herself. The black grandmother, for example, said she would have been *ashamed* if someone had come and found her grandson raping her.

Feelings for the offender can run a gamut from scorn ("You can't get it any other way, you got to do it like this?") to a sort of terrified pity. One young woman who noticed the man's hand trembling as he threatened her with a knife, put her palm to his cheek and sought to reassure him. "Don't worry, everything is going to be all right. I'll do exactly as you say."

The prolonging of a rape event is due to two principal reasons: the man is loath to use brute force and seeks to maintain the atmosphere of a compelling seduction, for which he will feel no guilt; or, once his controlling position is established he wishes to prolong its pleasure. Often the victim plays a useful, complementary role in either situation, for she neither resists outright nor acquiesces, so that during the extended scene the two explore a large range of male-female interchanges. There are occasions when, particularly if the offender is very neurotic and in need of supplying excuses to himself, he talks a good deal to the victim about how bad his own life has been and how he has suffered at the hands of women. This seeking of sympathy may disarm the woman into believing for a few moments that a balance may yet be restored, that all is not lost and that she may be able to salvage not only her own sexual integrity but a human relationship from this dehumanizing scene. Instead of making an all-out effort to escape she drops her guard and tries to find an amicable way of withdrawing and ending the affair—to no avail. Attempts to obtain the man's sympathy by speaking of her own life or problems are quite useless. The man is not interested in her as a person, even less in hearing excuses for not achieving his aim.

At the other end of the scale from the offender who seeks sympathy from his victim is the one who uses every means, including verbal ones, to humiliate her. The man who raped the librarian told her, "You are possibly the worst cock-sucker in the world." There is also the offender, who consumed by his neurotic needs, swings between the two extremes in a matter of minutes, changing from a raging animal into a whimpering, penitent but sly child, who nevertheless keeps a sure grip on his victim's presence. One offender who used a knife to hold a woman for six hours in his camper alternated his six rapes of her with spells of praying.

The offender who enrages his victim perhaps most of all is the one who is calm and aloof, self-assured. His air of unruffled superiority and cool determination, more than anything else, puts a woman in serious mind of revenge, although at the moment, stupefied by her impotence, she may be incapable of sorting out the source of her fury.

How long the event lasts depends to a great extent on how safe the locale is. If it is the apartment of one of the participants, or a deserted beach or a car parked in an isolated spot, it can turn into an all-night affair. This can be true with a strange offender as well as one who is known to the victim. In one case of a man who entered a small apartment by a fire escape, the all-night relationship took on the nagging overtones of a deteriorated marriage. The man noticed diapers in the kitchen when he entered and his first words were "I won't hurt the baby if you'll be nice." The baby wakened, and began to cry; the woman said it was time for the eleven o'clock feeding. The man agreed to wait while she heated the bottle and gave it to the baby. He used her sexually, then asked for a ham sandwich. She had only tuna. He complained about this. When she walked past him in the kitchen, he patted her familiarly on the buttocks. After eating the sandwich he insisted on sex again, then smoked a cigarette. He used her sexually a third time; then, quite at ease, fell asleep for several hours. On leaving he took a small transistor radio, a watch, and her money.

In another all-night-long event the offender, the son of a prominent physician, offered to drive a young woman home after an evening of bridge at the home of a college classmate. The victim, a virgin, was wearing her engagement ring, had talked of her fiancé who was working in another city. The ride detoured to a field where, after a long struggle, she was raped. Exhausted, they fell asleep, were wakened by daylight. There were no recriminations, no apologies. The young man asked to stop at his own house before taking her home. There, they found his parents pacing the sidewalk on that early Sunday morning. The mother asked the victim, "Would you like the doctor to drive you home?" Then she ordered her son to his room, and the twenty-six-year-old meekly obeyed. Clearly, it was not the first time this family had been confronted with such an event. The victim did not prosecute. When she arrived at her home, her parents also were pacing the sidewalk. She introduced the doctor by name. The family of the college classmate also knew that the couple had been missing all night; the three families had been in touch, but none phoned the police; in some circles such unpleasantnesses are not even discussed. The victim went immediately to bed and the event was never mentioned in her family again.

In the wrestling matches that can develop when the offender is unwilling to use his full potential for brutality, the victim can sometimes find within herself reserves of power she never knew she had. One victim pounded and struggled and rolled around on the floor for a full ten minutes before she realized that what was needed was to land a few blows on the neck and head where it would really hurt. Achieving some success in this, her mind cleared to the point where she realized that she could and should scream, which she did. This broke the spell, the stunned man exclaimed "Oh no!," gave up, and turned contrite immediately. The would-be victim found herself in a state of exhilaration over her new-found strength and self-determination that lasted for days.

Many victims by sheer grit and persistence have successfully resisted their attackers in struggles that lasted for hours. One young woman, attacked by two men while out sailing with them, jumped overboard, although their craft was miles from shore. They promised not to molest her further and she returned to the craft. When, however, their promises did not hold, she dived back into the ocean. Three times this was repeated until the men, frightened by her determination, which they feared might end in her drowning, begged her to come aboard, and took her back to land.

After a rape event, if the offender seems about to depart without harming her further, the victim's relief may be so great that her original fury and loathing are replaced by a feeling almost of gratitude. "He might have killed me and he didn't. I have my life."

The victim looks around at the world from which she was nearly cut off forever, stunned to realize what she has escaped. This experience of her own mortality, perhaps the first in an otherwise calm and uneventful life, is often the worst thing that has ever happened to her. It is not the sexual act, not even the violation of her sexual integrity which is the greatest shock to her, but this confrontation with a person who she felt was ready to deprive her of her life. All her pseudo experience in reading and seeing films has not really prepared her for this.

In the pampered world of women where often the only real blood she ever sees is her own benign menstrual blood, she is totally unequipped for the full meaning of bloody violence. Unlike men, who are reared in a tradition requiring them to be defenders of themselves, their women, and their country, with its full implications of win-or-lose combat, the female never envisions a struggle in which it is either her life or her opponent's. The idea of taking another's life is not only repugnant, it is utterly foreign to her, and to be faced with an opponent whose intent to win is so strong that he is willing to stake everything on it, even the ultimate act of destroying her, is so alien to all her knowledge that she has no psychic armor with which to respond. She has been bred to look to others for defense, to seek protection in other ways than by use of her own strength.

In this moment of truth, facing possible death, the victim may be astonished at what she deems her own moral failure, when her nature fails to deliver her the means to survive.

There are few events in a women's life to which she returns in thought more than to her experience of rape. Whether she is of a philosophic turn of mind or not, she ponders, questions, relives what happened for its meaning, its alternatives. Like most victims she may oscillate between exonerating and condemning herself, trapped in the conflicting views that society has given her about rape. As she examines her own part in the often long scene of the event, she considers the chances to act that she may not have used. Taking a lesson from this failure of will to act decisively in her own favor, she may come to a new grip on her choices as a woman. Particularly if she has psychotherapy, she may use the experience to adopt a new, self-determining stance, and can emerge from rape stronger than before.

Whether a rape event was of long or short duration can be of importance in the prosecution of the case, if the victim decides to take it to court. The defense attorney will in all likelihood try to use every possible turn of the story to prove that the victim was talkative, interested, tenderhearted, oblivious to means of saving herself, all of which will be construed as implied consent. The ladylike techniques she used to try to dissuade the offender may well be used to prove that she is a foolish, errant tramp.

8

It's Not Always Outdoors

MYTH: Rape is a dark-alley, outdoor crime.
FACT: Most rape takes place indoors, often in the home of the victim or the offender.

In the Philadelphia study, only 20 percent of the reported rapes took place out of doors. The rest occured either in the home of the victim or the offender or in another place indoors, except for 15 percent that took place in an automobile.

Whether a rape takes place indoors or outdoors depends to a large extent on where the offender first encounters the victim. If she is picked up at a bus stop, the rape is likely to take place in a park or some other outdoor locale. If their first contact is in her home or his, or another indoor place, it probably will take place there, although occasionally, if a party is in progress, the offender manages to lure the woman away from the group to the garden or car, where he carries out his intention. If he moves her against her will to an entirely different locale, an additional charge of abduction can be added to the crime.

Usually, movement is from outdoors to indoors, especially in the Northeast, where winters are bitter and snow covers the ground, although women have been raped out of doors even under these circumstances. One of the most striking facts about rape events is that they are so often carried out under what seem to be insanely unpropitious surroundings, neither safe from discovery nor at all comfortable. Some victims are not even fully penetrated because of the unnatural position in which they are assaulted.

In one third of the Philadelphia cases the offender met the victim at and committed the crime in her home or the place where she stayed. These cases included both the stranger (often a burglar) and the friend or acquaintance. Frequently other members of the family were there at the same time, either sleeping or working, or, if they were not at home, were apt to return at any time. The unreasoning urgency with which the event is carried out may convince the victim that the offender is acting out of desperate sexual need, which she may construe as a mitigating factor: "He couldn't help himself."

Some of the indoor places that have been seized for use include air-raid shelters, school buildings, garden sheds, vacant houses or half-completed constructions, the hallways and cellars or storerooms of apartment buildings, garages, and stores. One man managed to rape two women on the floor of a coffee shop restroom. He approached them at their table, asked if he could join them. Later when they went to the restroom, he followed them, pulled out a pen knife and threatened to cut their bellies. Lying on one, with his knife on the belly of the other and his feet braced against the door so no one could come in, he raped both before two other women arrived and began to shake the door.

One Philadelphia woman was raped in her home on three different occasions, about a month apart, by the same offender. The third time, the woman asked the man how he'd managed to enter since all the doors were carefully locked and nothing seemed to be forced afterward. The man said "I'll tell you when I leave," which he did. He showed her a defective screen he had discovered, and in fact showed her how to repair it.

Where the event takes place has been viewed as important in trying to determine whether there is more brutality to the victim indoors or out of doors. It was assumed that an offender would be likely to act with greater violence, to subdue her quickly, if they were out of doors and her cries could be heard by passersby. Or, conversely, in a building where neighbors could react. The issue seems to elude generalization and what happens seems to depend chiefly on what the offender thinks he can get away with. In her own apartment the victim may be too repressed or frightened to cry out, or the offender may know that even if the screams were heard, the neighbors would be unlikely to respond. In congested ghetto areas, especially in the summertime, windows are open and radios are playing, babies crying, families fighting, whipped children screaming, neighbors shouting and stomping up and down the stairs, and television sets blasting melodramas of violent crimes; then a few frightened screams, hastily cut off, would produce no results at all. There is so much noise of a violent nature on television these days that even in more affluent neighborhoods almost any unexpected cries are assumed to be from an overly loud TV.

On the other hand, screams in a public place may or may not produce results, since stories have been circulated about screams used to decoy would-be Samaritans in order to attack *them*. Many frightened citizens, in spite of themselves, are adopting policies of total uninvolvement: screams are other people's problems.

Besides the violence needed to subdue the victim there is also unnecessary violence: prolonged, sadistic banging around by an offender on a power trip. This, and the use of humiliating sexual practices, can take place only in a relatively secure place. One man, after drinking in a bar with a woman he met there, pushed into the car with her, produced a knife, and forced her to drive to a flat and isolated area near the airport. There, on the ground, he forced her to submit to anal intercourse. Disturbed by her crying, he turned her over and beat her, then forced her to have oral intercourse, including swallowing the semen. He took her back to the car, drove around aimlessly for awhile, then returned to the same place, again beat her on the face, insisted on anal intercourse again, then raped her face to face.

Moving from one place to another can serve several psychological purposes besides arranging for the security or comfort of the event. It can also be a way for the offender to test his influence over the victim, and it gives him time in which to strengthen his determination and intention.

The manner in which he secures the victim's acquiescence is often related to the place of the rape. In the all-night rape event that was like a deteriorated marriage, the woman was made to fear for the well-being of her baby. Victims have been seized off a sidewalk in full daylight with observers assuming that the woman's feeble attempts to shake off the man were part of a quarrel between husband and wife. The victim of the pair-rape that included her former lover did not try to run out during the few moments when she could have escaped because she was afraid the men would trash her apartment. There was also another illogical reaction—"If my very own nest isn't safe, then where *can* I go?"—like a horse unable to leave a burning stable.

Offenders have obtained consent in a parked car by tearing off the blouse and bra of the victim, and sitting on them. The victim, trapped in her humiliation and prudish guilt, is unable to leave. ("It would look as though I went halfway and changed my mind.")

The car not only provides access to victims and a means of escaping from the scene of the crime, but in its American version also provides the location for carrying out the event. European cars are less convenient for this purpose. A Volkswagen or Deux Chevaux is just too cramped for anyone but midgets, and, in fact, in Europe rape is committed in cars far less often than in the United States.

Many people's lives are so intricately connected with their cars that the car becomes a sort of second residence for them. Their thoughts, purposes, and destinies are so intertwined with their position in the seat behind the wheel that the car becomes a sort of alter ego, completing their personalities. It is their crutch, toy, image purveyor, and "equalizer." Its importance to youth, on whom the phallic symbolism of the long, thrusting hood is not lost, cannot be overestimated. The car can be a source of womblike comfort to women who retreat to it to flee the chaos of their homes. In one bizarre attempted-rape case, a woman walking in her sleep left her home to sit in her car, parked on the street, presumably because she felt more natural sitting there than anywhere else. A man who observed her night dress and dazed actions, assuming she was drunk, entered the car and attempted to assault her.

Many women have been assaulted in supermarket parking lots by men like One-Eyed Charley, and in fact rape crisis centers constantly warn women to lock their cars each time they leave them, or, if the car cannot be locked, to check it carefully before entering. More than one housewife, on her way home with a load of groceries, has been terrified to have a man rise up from hiding in the floor space behind the front seats, and force her to a deserted area where she was raped. Couples parked in lonely places have been attacked by two or more men, although sometimes one armed man is enough. These attacks can be particularly brutal, the woman's companion being knocked unconscious or tied up during the rape, which is often savage beyond all explanation, except that the security of the place permits it.

While the streets are still not a safe place for a woman to be, statistically fewer sexual assaults are committed there than in her own home. The myth of rape as a dark-alley crime proves once again the untruth that the woman society most esteems will be safest if she obeys society's rules.

9

It's Not a Secret Desire

MYTH: Women cherish a secret desire to be raped.
FACT: Women may fantasy rape, but this does not mean they desire it.

Amir says, "I don't believe any of the women I interviewed wanted to be raped." Some said ruefully. "I was foolish . . ." Others, in puzzled anger, complained, "If he'd been nice . . ." But all in one form or another showed the shock and outrage of the true victim.

Like most myths, that of rape as a secret desire has survived because of its usefulness to those who support it. Clearly, it was fabricated by men to excuse their conduct when they force women. The idea is a contradiction in terms. Then why does it persist? Does it contain fragments of real truth?

1. There is an enormous amount of fiction, written mostly by men, that seems to prove that women need to be pushed sexually. Books, movies, and television programs present the scene with wearisome regularity: an angry or stubborn woman is roughly seized for an embrace, she fights briefly, then her arm steals around his neck, her fingers begin to knead his back. This is not rape but a romanticism of the macho philosophy on which rape is based. Resistance turns to acceptance, then desire. A little force soon reduces the woman to oozy responsiveness. The invidious implied corollary is that *without* this show of force her sexual feeling would not develop. Ergo, women secretly desire rape because only force unlocks their sexual feelings.

2. A dismaying number of women still support the cultural image of a submissive female in thrall to a preemptive male. This continues to provide a substantial basis for the idea of sex as a male prerogative. (Sex is something men do to women.) Rape is only the

logical extension. If women openly accept the one, it is assumed that they secretly desire the other.

3. Women's sexual fantasies, according to those who have studied them, often include fantasies of rape, or acts that have certain elements of rape. The meaning of these not unpleasant images is worth a full discussion later.

4. "Stolen melons are the sweetest" (another half-truth) is the male version of the rape fantasy. Men who enjoy fantasizing rape, even if they don't act it out themselves, clearly have an interest in perpetuating the idea that what they like is also desired by women.

5. It is an established psychiatric fact that there are some masochistic women like Belle de Jour who prostituted herself and posed in a white gown for men to sling mud at her. Such women do seek pain and humiliation. But these few do not represent a truth about all females any more than a sick sniper picking off victims from a tower represents the truth about all males.

6. The Mary Magdalen complex. Believeing that the rapist is a man beset with uncontrollable sexual desires, the woman with a Mary Magdalen complex pities him and imagines that she, in her feminine generosity, could sacrifice herself to such a tormented man. She writes letters to convicted rape offenders or in other ways expresses a sympathy for the crime. Her neurotic behavior may seem to suggest that she cherishes a secret desire to experience rape, but as with the Belle de Jour type, this small group of women does not represent a truth any larger than itself.

7. The failure of women, in case after case, to give wholehearted resistance to an attacker cannot be dismissed as mere physical helplessness or justified prudence. This will be discussed more fully later.

8. After a rape case has made headlines, occasionally other women present themselves to the police and say that they have been raped by the same man. This "me too' reporting has been used as evidence that women are so excited by the idea of rape that they pretend or convince themselves that they have been victims also.

Actually this is not very common; delayed reporting occurs more often with child molestation cases than with rape. The parents of a child remain silent because they don't want to increase the trauma for the child and the rest of the family. When someone else takes action they want to give support, and so they speak out, late.

As to why "me too" rape reports exist at all, some may be bonafide cases, even if too old to provide a basis for prosecution. Others may be the kind of pathetic stab for attention that lonely folk make in a community that seems to give them no recognition.

The phenomenon of the not uncommon fantasy of rape might best be approached by understanding the place that rape holds in the vocabulary of human emotions. The act is loaded with strong and contradictory symbols that pull on both the male and female unconscious.

The fears relating to sexuality are among the most universal and profound experienced by humans. Males fear sexual inadequacy, symbolized by castration, and females fear sexual attack, rape. (Men too, fear rape, although it is primarily the woman's trauma that is of concern here.) These fears are archetypal and are found in every culture and epoch; they are traces of lifesaving instincts from man's most primitive period. Individuals become aware of these fears when they emerge in dreams and fantasies.

Fantasies, or daydreams, serve an important purpose. In sleep the Rapid Eye Movement time, which corresponds to dreaming time, has been found essential to the individual's well-being. Fantasies are believed to serve a similar purpose of reconnecting important circuits for the individual's psychological and somatic health. They mitigate boredom and anxiety; they provide useful, natural alternatives to a worrisome existence. Sometimes fantasies are of the yearned for, the denied: wealth, power, success. At others, in a morbid turn, they may be of ruin, pain, and death, so that the return to reality by comparison is pleasurable. In either case they serve practical and healthy functions in human experience; they add *change*. And they do this without shattering the pattern of reality. This is important, for often a real change is neither desirable nor possible.

The idea that women may fantasy what they don't want is easier to explain than male chauvinists might believe. Fantasies generally deal with material that is close to one's real life, although sometimes disguised. A woman may fantasy rape because she has strong sexual desires but can't believe she deserves a tender, caring experience. Her sense of unworthiness requires that she associate pain and humiliation with her pleasure in order to have it at all. If so, it is probably an old and familiar state, established in childhood, where most emotional roles originate.

Dissatisfaction with a sexual partner who is mousy and indecisive in personality or inadequate physically in sex might provoke compensating dreams about another, more virile partner, or a stranger. Or a sex fantasy might have a quality of vengeance toward one's partner—"If you don't act the complete man, I may fall into the arms of someone who is!"

The revenge may be more subtly directed against society by the prude who has been taught that feminine pleasure is indecent, so she must look to a rape fantasy for guilt-free fulfillment. "How can you say I'm guilty of being wanton when I'm lying here in chains?"

Fantasy often contains the germ of a true wish. Females who, in the puritanical tradition, have been denied the right to show sexual feelings can find in a fantasy of rape the pleasure of these feelings without being responsible for them. It is this rare element of abandon, rather than the fear or force, that is desired in the imagined act. Traditionally girls are taught that they must keep the control in a sexual confrontation "because girls have less feelings than boys." For generations mothers have warned daughters, "All boys want to; it's the girl who decides how far it will go." The true wish of a rape fantasy is the desire to give up control, to escape responsibility in an abandonment to the feelings so commonly denied.

While the *material* for fantasies is derived from current and adult experiences, the roots of fantasies are much older: they spring from infantile sources. However mature and sophisticated an individual may be, however rich and elaborate his or her fantasy, it is derived from the needs and experiences of childhood, usually before the age of three.

Each psyche interprets rape, as it does any strong human act, according to its own infantile experiences. The meanings of rape, therefore, are as nuanced as the images in a Rorschach inkblot. One woman talks about her fantasy of a *kind* rapist. In her daydream, he takes her very decisively, he ties her hands and feet to the bed, but she knows that she gives him great joy and this gives her joy too.

Most women, when questioned, admit that the most satisfying element in a fantasy of rape is the pleasure of helplessness. "I imagine I am weak and defenseless as a child, I am at his mercy . . ."

This feeling of helplessness is not so strange when one understands that it has its roots in the little girl's image of her father, who is the source of her knowledge of what a man is. Daddy is demanding, all-powerful, capable of terrifying, but toward her in her small helplessness he is kind, and a source of happiness. Daddy makes his little girl obey. He scares her with the absoluteness of his authority. His towering figure is bent on, he says, "your own good," even if it is unpleasant, like spinach. Daddy, although scary, is basically benign, even if he forces medicine or inflicts pain in spankings; a little girl wants to be close to Daddy.

Fantasies fill an emotional void; they are an attempt to work out unfulfilled needs. Since many little girls have incomplete, unsatisfying psychological relationships with their fathers, it is not surprising if in adulthood they fantasy a coerced form of love that parallels childish experiences, like Daddy insisting on a good-bye kiss soon after punishment.

In rape, the sex act, which is symbolically a benign state—two people in the ultimate act of closeness—presents the same contradiction with its pain and coercion. To a woman who has never experienced the real danger and fear in rape, a fantasy of it may parallel near-forgotten, not unpleasant memories of childhood.

The Freudian incestuous dream supplies further impulse for the rape fantasy. Teen-age girls pass through a stage of desiring their fathers sexually. When they are small, Daddy is the first male object of their love; when sexual feelings develop, they tend to attach first to him. He is a natural choice for a sexual experience. Freud found that teen-age girls frequently fantasied that their fathers attacked them sexually. This was a means of achieving gratification without the guilt of an overt act. It was also a mechanism for chastizing themselves for their wicked thoughts. The rapist fantasied in later years is the disguised attacking father figure: desired and feared, taboo yet irresistible, he must take by force that which can never be permitted. The phantom of the rapist is likely to be derived from the ill-perceived, haunting figure of the childhood image of father.

Violence, or threat of violence, is one of the principle elements of rape. It would be foolish to pretend that there does not exist in every human being, male or female, a little leap of response to witnessed or imagined violence. It is exciting; it releases a satisfying shot of adrenalin into the system, heightening all responses and making the individual more keen and active. A fantasy containing elements of violence may be, then, an alternative to a basically satisfying and stable relationship when an adventurous spirit craves a change, the opposite of her considerate partner. Although she would do nothing to shatter the pattern of her life, she finds a moment of pleasure in a harmless dream. This kind of fantasy is more common among stable people than is usually supposed because stable people are not given to discussing their emotional states; they don't have a need to pick them over, like last week's garbage, as do people who are locked in a constant struggle with neuroses.

A fantasy of rape or violent sex can also be an attempt to compensate for what a woman perceives as an inadequate sex life. She may imagine a man with enormous organs, or many men—a gang of construction workers—panting, grimy hard-hats—waiting to take their turn. As women become more sure of themselves sexually and more vocal about their rights, increasing numbers of them are complaining about the quality of sex they have been getting. It is now clear that an appalling number of men are terrible sexual performers and never guessed it because their timid partners pretended everything was great. Now that women are less concerned with "keeping a man," in fact, are examining their lives and considering whether a man is really worth the day-in, day-out trouble, a quick, unfeeling bounce in the hay no longer passes muster. Men are being judged on actual performance, and the roar from the locker rooms seems more and more to be all sound and fury, signifying little.

In fantasy the rapist is generally a superman, not so much violent as dominating and supersexed—able to give lots of what the dreamer may have not been getting in only frustratingly small doses. If she is unable, even in fantasy, to endow her real partner with the qualities she desires, she may fantasy a stranger. Sexual relations with a stranger are not permissible; therefore he must be so dominating that she has no choice but to submit. So what is the fantasy? A shadow, supersexed, aggressive stranger. The common image of a rapist.

When she fantasies rape, or violent sex with a stranger, the woman creates a powerful, virile image, which is in itself an assertive act. She endows the image with a strength and energy that cannot exist except as elements of her own nature. The dreams of a truly passive and unresistant female tend to be of a limply romantic nature: someone "being nice," touching her, confessing love in an ambience of soft lights and flowers.

The woman who fantasies a dynamic image is basically a dynamic personality; in a fantasy of rape she can enjoy a temporary change in roles although she would probably be furious if such a helplessness were forced on her or she had to pretend the role for very long. The desire to be utterly submissive, to experience a man who is overpoweringly assertive, is no more bizarre for a woman than the correspondingly common male fantasy of sexual passivity: the pasha and his harem. Minimal effort for maximum satisfaction. To be smothered in sensual attentions, to suffer from a surfeit of sex—this, to the man for whom life seems an unending hassle, is the ultimate dream.

For men, the fantasy of raping, although the exact opposite of the harem in psychological content—maximum effort for results that are unlikely to be outstanding sexually—is still one of the most satisfying. Aside from the male's vested interest in imagining that what appeals to him has a corresponding charm for women, the suggestion of enhanced power and sexuality is too potent not to have a nearly universal charm. Like the woman, the male may not have any desire to *experience* his fantasy; his sex habits, like his life, may be polite and easygoing. Still, the invidious and persistent message of the entertainment media today is that not only men but women enjoy this kind of sex. Television not only *replaces* most of our fantasy life, it tells us, through the reinforcement of repetition, and with an implied cultural support of its images, what one *should* fantasy.

The movies, written and produced mostly by men, are no less oriented to violence in sex. Three recent films, *Dillinger, Last Tango in Paris*, and *Blume in Love*, portray coerced sex in which the female isn't really angry even when, as in one case, it ends in pregnancy.

The most important difference between a fantasy of rape and a desire for the real experience is the element of control. In the fantasy, although it may seem to be a paradox, the helpless victim actually controls the acts of the offender. He may do this or that unspeakable thing, but he does them, so to speak, at her command. The aggression is basically the woman's, even if she relegates her own image to one of passivity. She has the pleasure of initiating the acts, while seeming to conform to the female role of submissiveness. Even if the scene is masochistic, it takes place within the framework of her own desire. The fear, if any, is simulated and safe; it can be compared to that of pretending to drop a child to make him shriek with pleasure. The rough stuff is containable and of the kind she fancies—maybe taped wrists and a paddling—but not heated coat hangers. Real terror and uncontrolled pain are not experienced in these fantasies.

The wish to remain in control and the fantasied role of victim are not really as incompatible as they seem. One can entertain a gratifying fantasy of dying and being mourned, for example, then leaping to safety—outraged at the heedless driving of a taxicab.

A last type of rape fantasy to complete the gallery of psychological elements is the dread fantasy. There are women who dread rape so much that they fabricate it. Obsessed by their dread, peeping in closets and under beds, these lonely, emotionally precarious women can, on occasion, convince themselves that they have really suffered the ultimate horror. Rape represents much more than itself: their shadowy terrors may mean fear of men, or fear of a knowledge of sex, but could also represent fear of touch, fear of dirt, of strangers, pain, night, and the unknown. Or a childishly potent combination of several of these and other elements. One theory is that conscious fear represents an unconscious wish and the intensity of the fear parallels the intensity of the desire. The underlying, deep, lost desire would be the need of love, touching, and human experience, especially with the opposite sex.

In a fantasy of rape, then, many complex elements are involved: archetypal fears, symbols, roles established by society, and one's personal needs and desires. But the emotional content for the fantasy always springs from visceral though near-forgotten experiences of childhood, re-staged with adult material.

What the woman experiences in the fantasy is therefore nothing like the real act of rape, but the satisfaction of working out old and primitive impulses to control and be controlled, with the contradictory element of having closeness and pleasure whether she wants it or not. Forced pleasure—the idea of having no alternative to enjoying one's self—is a childish sort of nirvana.

How can one deny that rape is not a secret desire among the women who seem to invite it by placing themselves in highly vulnerable situations? What about rape as an unconscious desire? When women hitchhike late at night, leave a bar with a man they have just met, or take other hair-raising chances, aren't they "asking for it"?

The reasons for imprudent behavior on the part of women are as many and varied as the reasons for the men's acts in this complicated crime. Sometimes it is foolish bravado: "Maybe it won't happen to me." Or unconcern: "What have I got to lose? I'm on the pill." Or defiance: "It's my right. If anything happens, it's the pig male who is guilty." Or silliness: "It's a way to meet people; maybe Mr. Right will come along." It can become a reckless life-style, a bad habit. Occasionally hitchhiking may become a necessity, if a car breaks down or runs out of gas, for example, but the female who really wants to protect herself can usually avoid such a mishap.

What about the unconscious desires of the "hussy" who deliberately flirts, then fails to deliver what her teasing suggests she is ready to accept? Here it seems that errors arise from the differences in male-female maneuvers. Even if seductible, the woman often has more complicated and longer-range expectations. The man's error lies in seeing her flirtation as asking not only for sex, but sex *on his own terms*. The problem, then, is a difference more in time and technique than in goals, a failure to permit the woman to decide "how far how fast," which she esteems her right.

The fact that women often have not put up wholehearted resistance to rape has been used to show that "they only pretend they don't want it—they really do." Victims flail and slap aimlessly; they wiggle and plead or turn utterly passive, unresisting as a corpse. They have even been known to cover their *heads* and wail; time and again they fail to make a determined effort to fight off an attacker. The young woman who was raped by the friend of her college classmate after an evening of bridge wrote musingly of her inability to harm him, in spite of what he did to her. "I had my thumbs on his closed eyelids. My hands were strong, I'd done a lot of ceramics. With one gesture I knew I could gouge out his eyeballs. I thought about how it would feel to my thumbs and to my stomach to make that gesture, and I couldn't do it. I thought I'd rather face V.D. or pregnancy than having to live with the memory of that. He had said, 'I'll kill you if you scream again,' and there was no doubt in my mind that he meant it. I considered half blinding him, but I knew that was no good. If I didn't *totally* incapacitate him he would kill me. I was a virgin. I felt terribly humiliated and defeated, defeated as I had never felt before. But even pregnancy, if allowed to come to term, seemed temporary compared to blindness for life. I remember thinking it out very clearly and making the decision."

Why do women have these built-in considerations for men, these paralyses of will with respect to their own well-being? What is this female impotence that is often taken for female masochism? Later chapters will deal with woman's physical ineptitude, her psychological inertia, and historical castrated social role. There are many reasons why a victim finds she is unable to defend herself; only someone who has no acquaintance with the female psyche could use this as proof that she desires rape.

Men want to believe their women are chaste. This desire, firmly rooted in their vanity, historically springs up from the tradition of primogeniture. The legend built up around chastity required establishing a kind of sexlessness on the part of women, in order to maintain it. If men admitted that women were as sexually motivated as they, then they could not demand chastity, for they had no intention of harnessing their own sexuality. They could demand purity and faithfulness only by convincing both themselves and their women that it was "not much of a sacrifice since women don't want or need sex, anyhow."

When men speak of "women's secret desire for rape" it is a subterranean acknowledgment that women have more sexuality than is being expressed, and that it has to go somewhere. It is an admission that the old legends have failed, and that the alternating scare and pamper techniques that have been used for centuries to try to turn women into sexless, compliant ninnies have not really changed a thing. The male double standard of sexual feelings is revealed for the fraud that it is, wrong—way wrong.

Gentlemen, look at the facts. Women can't be (1) *chaste and sexless* and (2) *desirous, not just of sex, but of RAPE*, at the same time. In the old days we might have said, "Make up your minds, which is it?" Now we're here to tell you that it's not for you to decide this important matter and in fact we have news for you. We are not chaste and sexless and neither do we desire rape. Are you ready for *that*?

In conclusion, be it known that: a woman may fantasy an encounter with a coarsely virile stranger, or she may dream a romantic version of rough or coerced sex. But this does not mean that she wants the real experience of rape any more than a depressed person fantasying an overdose of sleeping pills wants to have his throat slit. Experiencing rape, or even sharing the experience with a woman who has, is all it takes to separate the dreamers from the angry realists.

The dreamy innocent who imagines that rape might be exciting has never opened her bedroom closet on a sunny day and encountered a rapist who beat her about the face with one of her shoes. Nor has she been raped for an hour in a park with her little girl kneeling at her head, pleading, "Don't cry, Mommy, he might hurt you more."

If you want the truth about whether or not women really desire rape, ask a rape victim. No woman who has been raped will say yes.

II

THE VICTIM,
THE OFFENDER,
AND THE LAW

10

The Victim: Who Is She?

Unless fetishism is involved, any female, in theory, can be a rape victim, for the man who rapes does not seek a particular kind of person for his crime. Whether she is tall, rich, Latvian, musical, or wearing black garters is of no importance. The victim must have a female sex orifice and be vulnerable to him; that is all.

However, statistics show that some kinds of women are victims far more often than others. The most common victim is between the ages of ten and nineteen, and she is more likely to be black than white. Usually she has the same minimal education as the offender and is not skilled. Unemployment is not a related factor with her as it is with the offender, although her job may make her more vulnerable to becoming a victim.

Waitresses in restaurants, both black and white, are frequent victims. Highly visible to a large public, they can be singled out, watched, and approached with relative ease. They work hours that put them on the street alone late at night or early in the morning. Women who work in factories may have no more skill or education, but they are on the streets at rush hours and in groups. Waitresses in bars work late hours and alcohol is often a catalyzing factor in half-planned attacks. Bar waitresses are expected to be friendly, to create a congenial atmosphere; a certain familiarity and permissiveness of tone may be construed, especially where drinking has impaired judgment, as license to go further. Certain assumptions may be made about a woman because she works in a bar; in court, the fact that a victim had worked in a bar has been used as evidence against her.

Nurses work late and irregular hours; often they are on the street when no one else who is gainfully employed is around. Drunks, night

57

prowlers, and other suspicious characters are the only people about as these women in white stockings hurry through the shadows between the lights of the hospital and their homes.

Other workers providing services to the public, like shop clerks, car hops, dime store cashiers, cinema employees, and dance hall hostesses, add to the ranks of victims. Women who work in massage parlors would have a hard time proving rape, since they are generally regarded as prostitutes, although even if they are not the ambience of their work makes them vulnerable. University campuses are often used as hunting grounds; the young women in their peaceful, academic atmosphere are usually less on guard.

Rape by blackmail is so common in some professions that it is not even considered for reporting. There is the photographer's or artist's model who reports for work and is told that the job depends on accepting the preliminary hanky-panky. The aspiring young actress or dancer, show girl, or musician finds that the path to success must be paved with sexual favors to agents, talent scouts, T.V. personalities, movie directors, and male colleagues. In fact, she must yield, not so much in the hope of attaining favors as to avoid making enemies, for such are the assumptions of male privilege in these fields that to refuse can enrage a man of influence into permanent hostility. There is almost no job in which the advancement of a woman is not facilitated or deferred according to her responses to the sexual advances of the men around her. The coercion implied in the threat of failure makes these encounters a form of rape, in the feminine ledger, as much as that involving heavy fists. For the ambitious young woman has no real choice. If she wants to succeed she must swallow her pride and supply her body regularly, as rungs on the ladder up.

The secretary who is asked to stay late for a backlog of dictation and winds up on the company couch has been the subject of a benumbing dozens of jokes. *Esquire*'s readership was built solidly on the male perversion of the real facts into humor: the secretary depicted as a compliant, cotton-headed, pneumatic temptress, and the executive as a jolly old pop-eyed lecher. Too much shame, guilt, and economic loss are involved for these cases ever to become part of the public statistics, but acceptance of these roles and pressures forms the broad supporting base of the pyramid on which the more dramatic forms of the crime are built.

The rape victim is defined as a female who has been sexually used, against her will and without her consent. There are women, however, who although victims of the experience are not accepted legally as victims because they have a reputation for being unchaste.

Rape is the only crime in which the character of the victim determines whether or not the case will be pled. In no other legal proceeding is the character of the victim investigated before a complaint may be addressed to the court. The victim of embezzlement is not required to prove a perfect fiscal record before submitting his case. Nor must a victim of assault and battery prove his pacific nature. But the sexual habits and reputation of a victim are carefully scrutinized before her claim is validated.

According to Amir, and to other rape studies also, unrealistically low rape statistics—those that do not truly reflect the rate of the crime—often are due more to police reluctance to record them than to failure of the victims to notify the police.

There are four kinds of women who commonly cannot achieve recognition as rape victims because the police are unwilling to accord them the same legal rights as the rest of society. These are: the minority group woman (the black woman, the Puerto Rican, Chicano, or Oriental), the woman with a bad reputation, the hippy, and the prostitute.

The police were not interested, for example, in the case of an admitted derelict and wino who lived from one day to another through a makeshift sort of prostitution (she could be had for a glass of wine) when she was raped by a group of skid row bums.

The statistics on the number of black women raped are the highest in the land, so clearly there are vast numbers of these cases in which the evidence is so incontrovertible that, even if reluctant, the police cannot refuse to handle them. The general attitude, however, when a black woman appears at the police station and says that it was a black man who did it, is "Let them take care of it themselves." The notes made on the case are often cursory formalities with no real commitment to following through. The officers do not relish the hazards of combing black ghettos for an offender who probably could not be identified anyhow, since "they all look alike." Also, if blacks were encouraged to report, police would be besieged by accounts of black violence, and it would lower their efficiency records to have a flood of cases listed as unsolved.

The black cases most likely to be honored by police credulity and action are those of young girls, ten to fifteen years of age. The statistics on this group are so high that it is estimated that these girls are twelve times more likely to be raped than the rest of the female population.

Hippies present a complicated puzzle to the police, and attitudes toward them are a mixture of anger and uneasy contempt. Many of these girls are from the establishment families that the police are committed to protecting; yet these girls scorn the privileges of their class and expose themselves to the harassments of the lowest social groups. Theoretically then, they are to be treated with the same indifference as other low socioeconomic groups, yet the fact of their parents as potentially troublesome elements who might intervene remains. Police find hippy girls' attitude toward rape disconcerting, their manner often approaching something like composure. They are not vengeful and do not seek to press charges against the offender. Their concern is only that the facts be known, that the offender be listed, and that the case be added to the statistics of crimes against women. Often these young white women do not report rapes by black men, not for lack of personal indignation, but out of a higher moral sense that tells them that the black man's mistakes originate in an ethos that the white man's laws cannot yet judge fairly.

A fifth group that cannot claim the status of victim—and this is specifically defined by the law—is the woman who is raped by her husband. Since rape was originally defined and prosecuted as a form of theft, not from the woman but from the male to whom she belonged—her father or husband—rape cannot exist within marriage, for a man cannot steal from himself. It is not uncommon for a husband, during the wait before a divorce is pronounced final, to return to his wife and force himself sexually upon her. She may not, at the time, have pregnancy protection, which can be particularly unfair; pregnancies have resulted from such events. One woman, a devout Catholic opposed to divorce, was raped by her husband two years after he abandoned her and their child to live in another city with another woman. The wife bore a child as a result of the rape, and the husband, hearing of it, returned a year later to see the child and raped her again. Completely disillusioned by the failure of the legal system either to obtain support for the children or to stop her husband from molesting her, the woman obtained a divorce.

One last category of women who rate a low if not negligent position on the police blotter is the unattractive middle-aged spinster. Her complaint is usually dismissed as a sex-starved woman's fantasy, unless there is real evidence of brutality. The idea of the sex-starved female, which is the other side of the coin image of the female who is sexless until the man turns her on with a little pressure, is one of the most popular of male fantasies, and has served as excuse and rationale for a hair-raising assortment of male performances for many years.

Victimization is not a wholly random affair. The victim of a sex crime is usually one chosen from among alternatives. Something about her manner or her situation draws the offender to her rather than another. Although any woman can, by a fluke of circumstance, become a victim, certain types are statistically prone while others are only the exceptions. A millionairess *could* be raped by a disgruntled jockey in an empty stall while the horse was raced to victory by another jockey before a crowd of thousands; but the odds are against this.

The offender who wishes to rape a woman unknown to him does not look for a particular kind, but there are some women who appear to be more obvious quarry. Blonds seem more tempting, a blond waitress with a big bosom (whatever her face) is likely to be—and traditionally is—the target of more sexual flak than almost any other category.

There are certain attributes that work in the negative for the offender, hedging in his particular style. He may avoid certain age groups. Charley avoided teen-agers; some elderly bachelors are afraid of anything else. Many offenders work out of certain places and situations; whatever falls within the net there, it's all the same. The man who raped Langley Porter hospital nurses, although choosy about the broads he dated, did not care whether his rape victim was plump or a stick, pretty or with a face like the great bald eagle.

Victims are not special people physically, and victimization is not a pathological trait. But there are certain characteristics, given and learned, that seem to contribute to the event. The woman whose family life is unrewarding, who is ill at ease with her peers and generally dissatisfied with her lot in life, is more likely than a happy woman to become a victim. Often she is the female with a restless, unhappy look, a slightly run-down appearance, as if her self-esteem were low. Such women are ripe for exploitation, false promises, and naive hopes. They are psychologically less capable of defending themselves, and to the man searching for a victim they are marked as if with an X for their potential. Any woman who depends on others for her sense of self-worth, whose craving for attention from a male blinds her to the warnings in his flattery, is a ready candidate for the forced seduction that turns brutal. In line with the distinction made earlier, there are victims who are accidental and there are victims who create the circumstances for rape.

The female who grows up in a subculture that exploits women sexually and treats them as inferior beings generally has less chance to learn victim-avoidance techniques; she is less equipped to defend rights of which she is not sure. Thus a subculture can create types that are more prone to victimization. An air of meekness and vulnerability invites aggression.

Victimization can become an excuse for deviant behavior. Many women prisoners and prostitutes claim that they started their asocial activities because they were raped. Often their first sexual experience was rape by a member of the family or a close friend of the household. They go on to such crimes as theft—taking what is not theirs, since they have lost what is theirs—as a compensation for their own victimization.

One of the largest problems statistically, and thorniest legally, is that of the victim who is a minor. It is estimated that one fourth to one fifth of all middle-class girls become victims of sex offenses before reaching maturity. Among the lower classes the rate is even higher, between one third and two thirds. Each year in the United States about half a million children are victimized. The sexual offenses against middle-class girls are usually less severe than those against lower-class girls. Middle-class families make more constructive efforts to repair the damage done to their daughters; lower-class families are often unaware of the need for psychotherapy and do not have the money for it, anyhow. The amount of exhibitionism and pedophilia that takes place in the United States is impossible to estimate, but they are known to be extremely common.

In the Philadelphia study, as mentioned, fifty-one victims or nearly one out of thirteen, were under ten years of age. One victim, three years old, was taken from her crib, raped, and abandoned by the side of the house, near the window through which she had been removed.

Contrary to popular belief, it has been found that the child or adolescent victim may be a complicit if not an active participant in the sexual event. She encourages the offender through a neurotic need to "act out" ("acting out" being impulsive behavior that would not be indulged in if the individual realistically considered its consequences). The girl is often sexually precocious and quite pretty; she consciously uses her attractiveness to win attention from the opposite sex. While playing the sophisticated and provocative female she may find herself trapped in a situation from which she cannot retreat.

Often this child-vamp has an unsatisfying family background; she must look for love and affection elsewhere. Early she acquires a reputation for being impulsive and "easy." Her moods fluctuate; she is masochistic. During the event she may be submissive or may simulate resistance, but often she already has one or more sexual experiences behind her. Some of these girls begin as coerced victims, as in incest, but find it satisfying to continue.

Teenybopper, nymph of the slums and of the suburbs too, the Lolita of Nabokov's classic is a genuine little personality. Numerically these young temptresses are many and well known to the police and courts. It is not easy to decide what to do with a waif-courtesan who seeks in premature sex the tenderness she failed to find at home.

These girls are victims in the legal sense only; they have not the sense of pain and outrage of the real victim. In this situation, which is known as statutory rape, because the minor is not qualified to consent to sexual relations, the law conflicts with the victim's actual experience. The plot may thicken legally if the offender claims the role of victim by saying he understood the girl was of age. Then she becomes the offender, before the law.

There is also the minor who becomes a victim by accident. This girl is not provocative although she may be naive about avoiding situations with sexual overtones. With her, seduction, promises, threats, or violence, or a combination of any of these, may be used to accomplish the act. It is her first sexual experience. The offender is usually older and often already known to the victim. The younger she is, the less resistance she shows. If the molester is a stranger, the event is promptly reported to the girl's parents; there is more difficulty in reporting if the girl knows the man.

To complete the picture of the victim of the sexual attack it is fitting to note that the same traumatic experiences befall vulnerable men. In the gay world, unlit until recently, the same kind of exploitative violence takes place and the reactions are the same. Men are battered and forced at pistol point, the gun even used as an instrument. They are tied down, forced through humiliating acts. The rage and shame are the same, but there is even less comfort and support forthcoming from society; it is difficult to find a doctor who will testify as a witness to the injuries he is asked to treat.

The vulnerable, the defenseless, are always prey. In prison the older inmates gang up on the new arrival, rape him during exercise in the prison yard under the complicit eyes of the guards, who welcome this safety-valve behavior. Homosexual rapes have not yet been adequately studied although, since the sexual torture and murder of more than twenty-five youths in Houston by Dean Corll and his accomplices, investigation is clearly in order. Charges of sexual attack by one male or another are not listed as rape but in the less publicized category of sodomy. Often very young children are involved, as in the case of the four-year-old boy who was raped by a telephone repairman.

Behavior is visible, but experience is invisible. What degree of suffering must the victim experience to claim the title of victim? All victims have a sense of outrage or the experience is not rape. This indignation is increased if there is a great difference in the ages of the participants, as when a young man rapes a much older woman, or when assumed social lines are crossed, as when a man of one race rapes a woman of another. It is also aggravated when a woman is attacked by someone she has trusted, who she had assumed would respect her right to sexual self-determination. Rape is more damaging psychologically to a virgin; it is more damaging socially to a married woman.

Although taboos are frequently broken, there are permitted and forbidden victims in each culture. A woman may become one of these permitted victims through ignorance, naiveté, or self-destructive impulses. Any one of these reasons may be operating when a woman goes to a bar alone. In our culture, the bar is imbued with sexuality and masculinity. To enter a bar alone or even with another woman is to enter an atmosphere that is preloaded with overtones of intimacy and charged with anticipation. The woman is outside conventional female turf and is defying the proscriptions of her role. Certain assumptions are likely to be made about her character. She opens herself to being seen not as she sees herself but as others wish to see her. In this undefined territory, predicted and agreed rules of behavior no longer hold.

Whether the victim's manner is seductive or merely suggestive is not as important as how the offender interprets it. The victim need not do something inflammatory; she may become a victim by failing to do something. If a man believes a woman is teasing him, aggressive behavior will seem to him to be justified. For the "teaser" is a stereotype of low moral worthiness, a permitted victim. The woman may find she has little margin of freedom and maneuvering; in such a situation she finds her choices narrowed down to accepting sex she doesn't want, or facing violence. She may choose the first, to avoid the violence, then change her mind and report the event.

This is what is known as "victim-precipitated" rape. The woman may be what the court describes as "a reckless partner." She may have made mistakes, she may indeed not have acted in her own self-interest, but this does not change the basic fact that *a woman has a right to make her own sexual decisions*. Amir has interviewed women in every conceivable condition—weeping, battered, bleeding, distraught or in an icy state of shock, unharmed physically but white with rage—he has seen them all, but in his book, in spite of imprudence and addled reasoning, "There's no excuse. If a man forces a woman, it is rape."

There are men who maintain that rape is actually convenient for a woman; it eliminates the doubts and reticences that clog her mashed-potato brain. It *simplifies* her sexual life. It would be more accurate to say that it simplifies things for men who prefer to believe that women are incapable of desiring other than what men wish for them.

But if, as Pygmalion would have it, woman is designed by man's desire, why is she contaminated by these curious quirks of sexual reluctance? Or is that, too, part of man's design, since he is gratified as much by the conquest as by the sexual act itself?

It is a peculiar fact that, while women have incontestably strong feelings about their sexual rights, time and again they react with a disconcerting helplessness while these rights are trampled upon. The passivity of many victims, even mature women, defies all reasonable explanation.

One thinks of the nine Main Line society matrons, most of them probably capable hostesses and leaders in the community, yielding without so much as an overturned ashtray, according to the accounts of the garbage man, which the women did not deny. Even more incredible were the four women in the grocery store who stood obediently in a row and watched as first one and then another of their group was raped before them by the robber with the stocking over his face.

Baffled criminology texts discuss whether the female is apathetic, submissive, cooperative, contributive, or mitigating as a victim. Why doesn't she try to defend herself? Is it masochism? A primeval obedience to male physical superiority? Lack of moral fiber? What is wrong with her?

Women, it has been noted in different centuries and various places, are afflicted with a tendency to romanticize relationships, especially their own with men. They see roles for both sides cast in images of romantic antecedents. One of the most common for women is self-sacrificial in tone; the "masochistic postures" of women in romantic writing (done largely by men) are, when one thinks about it, striking. The helplessness and passivity sanctified in the literary models find their practical uses in an operating chauvinist society (there's no use going into a chicken-or-egg debate here), and the pattern is perpetuated.

One of the most prevalent expressions of the romantic impulse is The Encounter. Once, young women were warned, as they traveled or moved about in cities, "Above all, don't talk to strangers." Today young women, indeed women of all ages, travel and move about in cities for the express purpose of meeting strangers. The Encounter is becoming institutionalized in our culture; it is fast establishing itself as a social convention, in all classes and age groups, equaling in its satisfactions, if not status, the former uses of club and church as turf for meeting the opposite sex. Fraught with risk though it may be for the woman, more and more of them put aside inhibitions to try their luck. Meeting new people is fine, except that many of the feminine hopes and myths involved in The Encounter are a part of the murky psychology that is also responsible for the female's deplorable vulnerability. This psychology begins in prereading days, with Disney movies and the fairy tales foisted on defenseless tots in kindergarten. "Sleeping Beauty" is one of the most pernicious examples. Everyone remembers the script.

She is *lying* there in the middle of a forest, the ultimate in passivity—she's not even picking mushrooms or gamboling with elves, she's out *cold*. The Prince happens upon her, is ravished by her beauty (and passivity); he *kisses* her. He does not take advantage of her as she lies there, helpless under the spell of the wicked old witch; he only kisses her with such ardent but respectful devotion that she awakens, she becomes alive, she becomes *herself*, the real self that has awaited the magic kiss.

In this romantic scenario, which sets the tone for today's Encounter, one notices that this ultimate in tender lovers is a *Prince*, not the court jester or a splay-thumbed plumber. He is endowed not only with charm, and the noblest qualities of heart, but a kingdom. Sleeping Beauty's future is provided for. They find each other by *chance*, far from foyer and friends; they have no need of an introduction or credentials, they simply see each other and *know*.

These insidious elements conspire to make one of the most devastating of all attacks on female sexuality. The story implies that if you are utterly submissive, and of course beautiful and young, *fate* will deliver your Prince Charming, and the gloom, doubts, and inadequacies that have plagued your "unawakened" days will vanish with a kiss.

The fallout from this ruinous kind of fantasy often lasts a lifetime. The seductions, rapes, near-rapes, broken hearts, and warped marriages rooted in this insidious compost are without number. It is reinforced, of course, by the pandering tones of the soap operas, cinemas, and pulps consumed by young would-be heroines as they mature through pubescence to the day when they can leave home to try their fate in the city. Fervently these girls circulate, drink, improve themselves, read *Cosmopolitan*, swing. No matter how many or how disappointing the Encounters they have, the Holy Grail of that singular face, the dream of that awakening kiss and the transformed life beyond, remain the illusion that keeps them forever open and vulnerable. Old women sitting in residential hotels wonder how they missed it; middle-aged women weeping at *Love Story* think the film is realistic because it shows that life isn't always perfect afterward.

No stratum of womanhood is wholly impervious to the dreams supplied in the old childhood fables. Bewitched into irresponsibility, the victim of the Prince Charming myth abandons her fate to the chance glance, the magic greeting, the wave of a fairy godmother's wand. Instead of wresting her fortune from life, she abdicates to a passivity that undermines her whole personality structure. Derelict in her moral duty to herself, how is she to defend herself physically when the need is there? She may well become a statistic as a victim of rape.

11

The Offender: Who Is He?

What kind of man commits rape? Society's picture of the offender ranges from one extreme to the other. He has been thought to be undersexed and impotent, a half-man who could find pleasure only in hurting and humiliating a woman. He has also been depicted as an oversexed monster endowed with an extra set of testicles and a penis like a rhinoceros horn. Sometimes he is supposed to be a mental incompetent, unable to grasp the seriousness of his crime, at others a fiendish intellectual like the Marquis de Sade. At no time is he supposed to look like anyone you *know*.

Efforts have been made to establish the rape offender as a sort of insatiable Don Juan, thus supplying a romantic gloss to the image, although Don Juan's pleasure was to seduce women, not to rape them. Medical men have tried to explain rape in terms of physical symptoms, describing the seizures as "latent epilepsy," but there is no proof of this.

The rape offender who is fingerprinted and photographed at the police station is usually disturbingly ordinary. The crime is most often committed by men who are young, poorly educated, and of the lowest social and economic groups. In the United States these offenders are predominantly black and frequently unemployed. Often they have a record of arrests connected with violence before they are charged with rape.

Although this is the classical prototype predicted by sociologists, analyzed by psychologists, and studied by criminologists, the men who make up the rest of the statistics are of a rich diversity. Rape is chiefly the sport of the young, but there are also several kinds of middle-aged men who rape. One is the old bachelor who, because he is afraid of women his own age, attacks inexperienced young girls. The male menopause is now a recognized phenomenon. Occasionally it produces an offender who tries to prove he is still attractive through a seduction; the attempt fails, degenerates into rape. Another type is the bored husband who has become sexually lazy with his wife and casts around for a different experience, a new thrill. A variant of this is the split personality, a prosperous and responsible married man in his middle years who develops a weird second life sexually, patronizing bordellos and prostitutes and even resorting to rape. In one such case in Philadelphia, a white businessman with an impressive background picked up and raped a twelve-year-old black girl. The event seemed quite out of character for the man who was happily married and known to be of a meticulous nature, a perfectionist in his work.

Immigrant men who are without women and short on money and social status can resort to rape as a sexual outlet, particularly if the homeland's mores tacitly condone "the taking of women." One of Amir's cases involved three Arab men who said they hadn't enough money to go to a prostitute; they resorted to seizing a woman off the street.

Walking the streets of every major city in the land are other recognizable types: the Saturday night swinger who wants his "piece" and doesn't care how he gets it: if an easy seduction doesn't present itself he takes a shortcut. There is the "mad at the world" type whose rage is ready to be released on the most handy vulnerable object. If that object happens to be a woman, rape is what a man does to a woman. There is the down-from-the-farm hand who, as a change from sheep ("I stick their back feet down inside my boots to hold them") drags off the first woman who answers his "How ya doin'?" And the man who, with a buddy, carries off a pair-rape to shore up his image as a virile good fellow.

The kinds of men are as various as their psychological drives. Rage and frustration over a dead-end existence, sexual stress, miscalculations in role playing, a sick and anarchic self-image, hatred of women and particularly a loathing of one's wife, an almost innocent assumption of male sovereignty in sex—these are some of the factors that precipitate the slow or swift moves to seize an unwilling woman for sexual purposes. Rarer are such intellectualized reasons as Eldridge Cleaver's professed rapes of white women as an act of political revenge.

"A patronizing attitude" toward women probably best describes the psychological stance of the man who rapes. The two most common denominators of convicted offenders are a low I.Q. and a contempt for what they perceive as the inferior status of women.

Rape as a form of accepted behavior can begin at an early age. Boys as young as ten have been charged with rape. It is not necessary to discharge or even to sustain a long erection. If there is any penetration of the female he is guilty. Often these young minnows brag about their role in a gang shag and convict themselves. Most offenders between ten and fourteen years of age in Amir's study were part of a gang rape in which the victim had already been laid out by the older members. There were forty-seven in this age group in his study, almost as many as there were men over forty years of age.

Rape is commonly associated with alcohol, used by either the offender or the victim or both, but drugs are rarely present. Pot reduces aggressiveness and mobility, hash even more so. While muggings by junkies are common, unlike other robbers and burglars they don't linger to rape; they are in a hurry to get their fix. Besides, they are weak and sick; they have little sexual drive.

Is the rapist a man who has progressed from minor sex offenses, such as exhibitionism or voyeurism, to more serious ones? This was a theory that at one time justified harsh treatment of peeping toms and men who opened their raincoats in the park when young girls passed. But these men are generally shy, afraid of women. It has not been proved that this type transforms into an aggressive and brutal personality.

In appearance the stranger who rapes is no larger or stronger than average. Some are impractically scrawny and small, but compensate with a knife, gun, or stick. Often they are quite ordinary in appearance although they may be good-looking, like the Langley Porter nurse offender who found women a pushover, when he bothered to ask. One study tries to correlate physical defects with convicted rapists, but Amir found no evidence to support this. Admittedly, Charley of Oakland was one of nature's mistakes. Besides having only one eye, he was small, ugly, and crookedly hunched over, almost deformed looking. His teeth were rotten, his clothes filthy. He knew he was repulsive and frightened women; it added to his success. Although he did not have a record of violent offenses, he was known to police as a vagrant.

Charley had had only three or four years of school; he was almost illiterate. The average offender has no more than six years' education and even this does not mean much; he may simply have been pushed from one grade to the next without having absorbed the material of the first three grades. Because of poor qualifications at least one fourth of them are unemployed.

Even when he has a low I.Q. the rape offender often shows real cunning in finding and trapping his victims. If he is successful, he may develop a skilled modus operandi. One man posed regularly as a telephone repair man. Another said he was a County Health officer, checking women for breast cancer. Albert de Salvo, the Boston strangler who murdered thirteen women, claimed he'd raped dozens who fell for the ruse that he had been sent to make repairs in their homes.

Although the examining physician labeled him "retarded," the Main Line garbage collector was careful enough not to get caught while raping nine of Philadelphia's prominent matrons. He knew that these women did not have live-in maids but depended on help that came during the day. He entered their homes between 7 and 8:30 A.M., leaving before the help arrived. The back doors were unlocked for deliveries, so it was easy to walk in, after checking the garage to make sure the husband's car was gone. Although he continued in his normal rounds of collecting the garbage at his victims' homes afterward, he never tried to enter again.

Most men who rape are sexually mature. Although it may be a first experience for some seventeen- and eighteen-year-olds, most of them at this age have a history of a full and frequent sex life.

If it were possible to measure sexuality or sex drive, how would rape offenders rate? "Some of them are athletic," Amir notes dryly. The man who raped two women in ten minutes while robbing a grocery store with a stocking over his face was not alone in his feat. The man who raped two women in the toilet of a coffee shop was another, and many offenders repeat intercourse three or four times if they remain with the victim in a safe place for an hour or two.

On the other hand, in one pair-rape, one of the two men never did achieve an orgasm in spite of his long and angry efforts to do so. Some offenders, when they find themselves failing sexually, beg for help or, furious, beat the woman out of frustration. There are even cases of men who resort to masturbation, proof of a chaotic sexual pattern. One offender, convicted of twenty-five rapes in San Francisco and Marin County, did not sodomize his victim but lay on her back and manipulated himself against her bare buttocks. In spite of their aggressiveness, many rape offenders are sexual failures.

The man who rapes, in fact, is usually, one way or another, a loser. Infantile, angry, desperate to conceal even from himself how inadequate he feels, he is aggressive because he lacks better ways of communicating. Charley was afraid of young women; the garbage man said black women wouldn't have him.

Rape offenders are most often from the laboring class, between the ages of fifteen and twenty-four, and members of minority groups. Their victims have similar backgrounds. Seventy-seven percent of the offenders and their victims in the Philadelphia study were from minority groups.

The mores of each ethnic group are an important factor in the amount of crime its members produce, and whether or not the crime is reported. Four of the offenders in the study were Puerto Rican. In Philadelphia, the Puerto Rican community, unlike the one in New York City, which is riddled with drugs, is on the way up the social and economic ladder. Rape has a special place in the culture: it is used by young men to get a woman to marry and therefore often goes unreported.

Some immigrant groups have rarely contributed to rape statistics. The fire and brimstone threats of Catholicism held the young Irish blades in check; in their church rape is a mortal sin. Among Italians, also Catholic, religious prohibitions are less strong. Rape, when it occurs, has overtones particular to themselves and is handled within the community. Orientals almost never appear either as offenders or victims. The Chinese horror of any involvement with the police is expressed in the proverb "Better to tangle with the devil than the police."

The blacks of America are involved in rape more often than any other minority group for reasons that are easy to understand. Their religious restraints against sex are not as strong as those of the Irish; sexual activity is viewed with greater tolerance. But of even greater importance are the uses of violence in the pattern of their subculture. Blacks raised in the hard life of the ghetto learn that they can get what they want only by seizing it. Violence is the rule in the game of survival. Women are fair prey; to obtain a woman one subdues her. In 78 percent of the cases in Amir's study, black men raped black women. In 12 percent of the cases black men raped white women. It is far more likely for a white woman to report interracial rape than a black woman, and the 3 percent found for white offenders of black women is no doubt derisively low. White men raped white women in 7 percent of the cases. In sum, for every reported rape in which the offender is a white man, there are nine by blacks. Black men, who constitute about a tenth of the U.S. male population, are involved in 90 percent of the reported rapes.

The sad statistics represent sad facts. The man who is the most frequent offender in violent crime in the United States is also the most frustrated. The pattern for the violence in which he so often lives began with the first roundup of slaves transported to the New World and has continued with chains, whips, and lynchings to the present decade. Attitudes have not changed much, in some places, if a car full of white men can still ride through a town in Mississippi and, as random sport, gun down a black graduate standing on the sidewalk with her diploma in her hands. For two centuries a legacy of hatred and repression largely unimaginable to whites has been the lot of the majority of blacks in this country. Within their own subculture they have learned to see things according to their own norms, the white man's norms having rarely proved applicable to them anyhow.

The age level of the U.S. black population is an important factor in rape statistics. Rape is predominantly a young man's crime, and more than half of the black people in America are under the age of twenty-five. Unemployment seems to be a contributing factor, or, at least, often is associated with rape. Fourteen percent of black men of all ages are unemployed and in some areas 40 percent of those under twenty-one are out of a job. Unable to prove himself in his work, the black man is often without status or authority. He resorts to showing his manhood through a sexuality that becomes hyperaggressive in rage.

He expresses this festering rage in the rape of his own women rather than whites. The black woman is closer at hand, and rape is largely a neighborhood crime. Many blacks never leave their ghettos; some have never seen the city outside, only a fifteen-minute walk away, and have no incentive to go there. In the psychology of the black family, the economic dispossession of the male weighs heavily. The woman can always work, at least as a domestic. The man has difficulty finding work that is not badly paid, or that he considers demeaning—when he can find work at all. He is angry that the woman has money and he hasn't; she is angry at having to support a man who can't work. She exercises her prerogatives with an infuriating disdain. Tensions between the sexes mount, explode frequently in acts of violence of which rape is one.

Many black children are raised in fatherless homes. If a male adult is found on the scene the welfare check vanishes. Since the welfare check is a more reliable source of income than a man, the woman opts for security; boys are raised in a mother-dominated environment. Their sexual aggressiveness is often a form of protest against black matriarchal rule. A furious revolt against the "mom" figure is implicit in the raping of the mother-in-law, described earlier.

In the case of the grandmother, the symbolism is even stronger; the man had been raised by her instead of his mother, from the age of eight.

Sexual aggressiveness is part of the subcultural pattern for working-class blacks. The young men look for thrills and achieve status through various kinds of aggressive actions, such as gang fights, crime, and sexual exploits. They display their masculinity in brief, explosive relations with women. Lower-class young black women usually enter into relations with men through sex, instead of such middle-class channels as clubs, school, and community affairs. For young girls, sex provides prestige and a chance to enter the boys' peer groups from which they would otherwise be excluded. In the American black ethos, aggressiveness and sexuality are closely joined with the elements of survival.

The rape offender with a low I.Q. is the most dangerous. Amir says Charley was probably more retarded than psychopathic, although he was the closest to being psychopathic of all those Amir interviewed. The term psychopath has become a mixed bag applied to many unexplained characteristics. Sadists are disturbed people, but that does not mean that they are psychopathic. Nor are all brutal people psychopathic. There is, for example, no psychopathy in gang rapes, although they may be extremely brutal.

An individual with a low I.Q., when possessed by an idea, seems driven by it; there is no place for nuances or alternatives, and this is what makes him particularly to be feared. This drive is often accompanied by the sort of premoral level of judgment that a child of the earliest years would show. He may take horrifying risks, the kind that only an unthinking toddler would hurtle into. This is not bravery. Consider the man on the way to the movies, stopping to rape a girl on the street. Consider the young man, not a student, who raped a Berkeley high school girl on the indoor stairway while school was in session.

Many men who dream about rape, however, when they start to put their ideas into action, find it more trouble than it's worth. At the first hitch in the plan they become frightened and bolt with their pants hanging down. Picked up later for attempted rape they are rueful. "Women are bitches. That's it. They're difficult."

Does the rape offender feel guilty? He knows rape is wrong, but the amount of guilt he feels depends on how mentally disturbed he is. Disturbed people can have a sense of guilt about what they do, even though they cannot resist doing it. Those who do not feel guilty are either retarded, or under the influence of a subcultural rationale, or the general male chauvinist rationale of "it's my right, and besides, women really like it."

Once the offender has been through the justice system he is more sophisticated the second time around. Often he has had group therapy in prison, can explain his motives in psychological terms. All the modern jargon and rationalizations are used: "deprived background," "male image," "unloved." Still, the men do believe their own excuses, says Amir. "Look, a woman wants sex, why does she resist?" complains one. "Women are fucking all over, why should they stop at me?" says another.

None of them ever expressed regret to Amir. They only regret getting caught. Some regret the beating, say, "I was afraid, I had to shut her up. I was afraid I'd get caught." In court they rarely if ever apologize for their actions. A few offenders have said to their victims, "Close your eyes, don't look at me." This is so the woman will be unable to give an accurate description of him or to recognize him in a police lineup. But shame is also involved. Some have worn ski goggles all through the rape. Amir does not accept the notion that there can be "good guys" among rape offenders. "If a guy can rape, he must be sick."

The man who rapes is a man who has a problem with women. Men are basically afraid of women, says Amir; women are an enigma. They are dangerous, they can seduce. A woman may be weaker physically, but she can get a man to do things he doesn't want to do, things he had no intention of doing. This is a power superior to physical strength. Men make abstracts of women, rather than taking them concretely, as they are. Then they show their fear of this abstraction by hostility. The general hostility to all women is intensified, for the rape offender, in the person of the victim when she resists him.

A strict father and a promiscuous mother may combine to produce a son who will rape. The boy gets the idea that women can't be trusted, that they are cheating, unworthy persons, and he adopts his father's "hardness" toward them. There is also the theory that sex criminals are brought up without fathers, reared by dominating mothers. This may produce homosexuality, or conversely a rape offender. Another theory is that of the seductive but rejecting mother; this is a superego Laocoon, based on an unresolved Oedipus complex. The son is unable to form a complete idea about his mother. She should be taboo, but she isn't, she's seductive. But not to him. With him she's cold and rejecting. Desperate for an affection that is confused with a desire for sex, the man acts out the impulses he has felt for his mother, who, because she is taboo, can be taken only with force.

Since such theories about human development are unprovable, they must remain speculations, like those about prostitutes, who are thought to be seeking the never-felt love of their fathers in the beds of many men. Or, conversely, because they hate men, taking their penises out of a penis envy that cannot be resolved in any other way.

Sometimes the victim will ask the offender, during the act, why he is doing it. Most often the answer is a curt "I don't know." Some are annoyed by the question, answer with a blow or a bark, "Shut up, bitch." Occasionally one will mutter what's on his mind, "I been pushed all over, my whole life." Some give a frankly sexual interpretation: "I was looking for a chick and you're the unlucky one." "Just needed a little cat tonight." One knowledgeable offender, anticipating the girl's worry, told her, "You can tell your boyfriend that it's not your fault; you have no burden to carry."

Men who rape have often been introduced to sex in a perverse manner. They do not feel sexually satisfied unless the act is deviant or violent. The struggle with the victim may be important to stimulate him sexually. This is one explanation of why offenders look for a victim rather than go to a prostitute.

"Relax and enjoy it," which was certainly coined by a man, is an example of the contradictions in the offender's manner of thinking. If he did not want and expect resistance, he would not rape; on the other hand, he does not really want *trouble*, and in fact would like the victim to show a little *appreciation*. "It's a fact that women have to be pressed a little; I can satisfy them, I can provide the opportunity." Another example of the involuted thinking: "Sex is for the male, so what I'm offering is a chance for you to enjoy it."

The idea of sex as a "game," of something to be won by a little effort, is still common to many men who could not be classified as neurotic. "Playing the game" may simply include using a bit of judicious force. This also makes them feel more "manly." Some men are helpless in a social situation, unable to talk to a woman. Unable to seduce a partner, they resort to action. The men who attack young girls tend to be impotent, unsure of themselves. This category often includes the elderly bachelor who, because of middle-class inhibitions, is afraid to go to a house of prostitution. He has the desire for sex, but is unsure of his sexual ability. He picks up young girls with what seems a grandfatherly interest, but the encounter deteriorates into molesting them. He is not violent unless they panic.

In prison, the men who have been sentenced for straight rape are regarded with sympathy by the others, who consider it a "bum rap." However, men who have been convicted of sexually assaulting children are held in such contempt that they often require special protection from the other prisoners. "Baby rapist" is one of the vilest of epithets, even in the underworld.

The act of rape is a contradiction in itself. In its brutality and contempt it is an expression of hatred of "the other," most particularly women. But it is also a crime of touch, in which the offender seeks the ultimate physical closeness to another human being. In a warped way, the man who rapes is showing a need for contact with another human being. His is not just a power play, or he would be content to manipulate people, directly or indirectly. Nor is it just a destructive urge, like that of the arsonist, whose target is an inanimate object. Nor is the rapist just exploitative, like a robber or swindler, looking for his own profit. Rape combines a sense of touch with all of the above elements. Whatever the offender's feeling for his victim—contempt, loathing, fear, or rage—the fact is that in his crime he seeks to rest in a moment of abandon inside a woman. To be inside a woman has been alternately interpreted as an act of victory and an act of surrender. While it is true that some offenders permit themselves the luxury of a momentary nap after completing the sex act, implying a certain trust or confidence, and there are cases in which the man shows ambivalence toward his victim, including the hope that she does not condemn him, it would be exaggerating to say that the offender has any real concern for her. The essence of the act is indifference to the woman's feelings.

Occasionally an offender will try to transform the event into a love affair. He will cover the victim, take her home, say, "You're nice," apologize. In a cynical maneuver he will try to transform the situation from impersonal to personal. If he succeeds, and the woman does not report it, the man scores a double success. He has had the desired experience, and he has manipulated the situation so that he is free to do it again. Success breeds repetition. Men who rape without getting caught repeat. Rape seems to become, if not checked, a bad habit.

Although the differences between an offender who is psychopathic and one who is criminally sadistic may seem a matter of degree, their psychologies are different enough to be of importance to the victim and to society in its treatment of them.

The psychopath is locked outside reality; he cannot be moved by the behavior of "the other"; he is unreachable. He is beyond pleasure, pity, fear, or satisfaction and sees all human activity as through the wrong end of a telescope, far away, tiny, and unrelated to himself. He acts compulsively, unable to judge his actions or vary his behavior, once it is set in motion. The psychopath is incapable of remorse, psychologists say. His feelings are sealed off in a watertight compartment; he strikes down his victim as he would a tree. Unable to respond to the humanness of others, he seems to be the blind-deaf automaton personified in the horror of a Frankenstein monster. Autistically impelled, he obeys commands from a center cut off from human input.

A victim who realizes she is in the hands of a psychopath whose "set" cannot be altered, may find the superhuman strength to fight or flee, the only alternative being to resign herself to her fate, which may include murder. Amir reports one psychopath who tore apart his victim's vagina and anus with his hands.

There is more hope for a victim who finds herself trapped by an offender who is a hard-core sadist. This man is still in touch with reality and susceptible to the human condition, however incorrigible he may seem. He is aware of the risks he runs and may derive extra satisfactions from those dangers. The pleas of the victim do not move him, he may even be stimulated to further violence by them. Still, he does react to his victim, even if negatively, and in this interaction there is always the possibility of altering the course of events. The clever victim has a chance to participate in the drama; she just may find a way to spare herself some of the unnecessary brutality.

The kind of compulsive, withered, despairing personality that resorts to rape is brilliantly drawn in Evan S. Connell, Jr.'s, *Diary of a Rapist*. The day-by-day record reveals a man whose bitter sense of inferiority to women is combined in a bizarre way with his conviction that even the best of women are whores, some are only trickier at disguising it. The reader watches the progress of his antisocial acts: cutting a hole in the back seat of a bus, stealing women's lingerie, entering homes at night, and finally the crime itself. This petty bureaucrat who cringes at his wife's reprimands, who is paralyzed by a look from a colleague at work, who refrains from growing a mustache because it might be considered aggressive and entered on his efficiency report, finally puts a knife to a girl's throat.

"She deserved it," he tells himself. "I was only the instrument in her just fate."

12

The Law: A Reflection of Old Prejudices

As a legal problem, the crime of rape is unique. It has produced some of the most emotionally charged, legally questionable, morally grotesque actions in the history of jurisprudence. Some of the heaviest sentences ever meted out to an offender by a court have been for rape: a thousand years of incarceration, death by hanging four times. In some parts of the United States the punishment has not awaited a court judgment but has been carried out by a vengeful mob, hastily and with flagrant sadism, the man presumed guilty usually being black.

If society is often exceptionally harsh in dealing with the rape offender, the status of the victim before the law is also unenviable. In a rape trial the burden of proof imposed on the victim is dual. Not only must she prove that her assailant is guilty, she must prove that she is innocent. Rape is the one crime in which proof of guilt of the offender depends on proof of innocence of the victim. The offender is assumed innocent, as in all legal proceedings, until proved guilty. The plaintiff, however, unlike other plaintiffs, is not assumed innocent but must prove it.

For the defense attorney, this innocence will depend on whether she meets the highest standards of chastity. If she can be shown to have had sexual relations with her husband before marriage this fact will be used to prove not only that she is unworthy of the court's time, but that she is of a lascivious nature and consented to the act with the offender, if she did not actually provoke it.

Because of its sexual aspect, and because it is a crime of violence, rape has the power to produce, in those who must deal with it as representatives of society, highly charged, judgmental attitudes. These strong emotions, once evoked, seem to need a target, to compel a clear-cut, punitive decision. Revenge seems required. It may be directed toward the offender or deflected to the person of the victim. If society or its representatives in the court do not find an easily defined villain in the rapist, then it is the raped on whom society's uneasy and angry feelings about mislaid sexuality are focused for release.

So difficult is it for the average victim to get a fair trial that plea bargaining is an accepted formula for settling a rape case. Often the agreement is for a plea of guilty to as few as one or two out of fifteen criminal counts, an acknowledgment by the plaintiff's attorney of the difficulty of prosecuting the crime "if the victim isn't a ninety-year-old nun with four stab wounds."

While in many states the court may examine the plaintiff's sexual past at length, on the basis that this exposition of her character is central to proof of the offender's innocence, the offender's sexual history cannot be mentioned. Even if he has a police record of numerous rape charges, this cannot be introduced unless the defendent takes the witness stand, which is rare.

Rape is a crime in which the offender finds a cryptic support for his act in the songs, jokes, folk tales, and traditions of a culture that gives a wink of admiration to the man who can do it and get away with it. Forcing a woman sexually is not a crime to many men.

Consider this remark, in a book on rape written by an M.D. (a male) in 1968: "Court dockets throughout the nation contain many a tragic reference to a case wherein a perfectly normal and inoffensive and even highly intelligent male may have succumbed just once to the dreadful allure of sexual violence."

In the court's assessment of the crime, historical elements, common myths, local traditions, current social customs, and individual prejudices play important roles. Often justice depends not so much on what happened during the event as on elements extraneous to the crime, and above all the peronalities of the two chief actors, as perceived by society. More than in any other crime the trial centers about the person of the victim.

Whether the case even reaches a court for trial depends on who the victim is. If she is one of several accepted victim types her complaint may be dismissed as unworthy of entry on a police blotter. If she commands the proper social connections her case can become a cause célèbre, producing reams of newsprint, exciting the passions of millions, and involving some of the most prominent personalities in the land, as did the Massey affair in Honolulu.

These extremes are merely an extension of the differences in attitude with which rape has been regarded, through the centuries, in Western civilization. Historically, rape has been either abhorred or ignored; either it merited the ultimate punishment or it was not viewed as a crime, depending on the position of the female in society. In biblical times rape was not an offense against the person of the woman, but against her father, if she was unmarried, for it represented a financial loss to him in bargaining for marriage. If she was already married, it represented a social loss to her husband and his family. Punishment of an offender was viewed as a reparation to the father or husband.

Rape became a social problem about the time that man decided that a woman's chastity was important to him, and chastity became important when man became concerned with the inheritance of property. As man's work was to provide a living for his family, the woman's work was to provide children, additional lives to help man in his work and to inherit the gains. Man wanted to be sure those children were his own. A woman was fit for this work only if she was chaste. Society judged man by his productivity, woman by her chastity. Society's attitude toward the man who fails to fulfill his role is reflected in its epithets: villain, wastrel, hoodlum, vagabond, ne'er-do-well, outlaw, bum. A "bad man" is one who harms others. A "bad woman," however, is not one who is wicked, but one who is unchaste. Society considers her bad if her role as a producer of heirs becomes questionable.

Chastity, like virginity, either is or isn't. There's no in-between, a woman cannot be "a little bad" or "occasionally bad"; if she's not chaste as a vestal virgin, she's a trollop in society's view.

Society's anger against a woman who fails to fill a chaste role is far stronger than that against a man who fails to fill his social role. A man can be rehabilitated if he is a rogue, a ruffian, a black sheep, a prodigal, or a rascal. But what can be done for a fallen woman? Has there ever been a fallen man? A woman who is improper sexually is loose, but a *man*? Has one ever heard of a *man* of easy virtue? A woman who is known to enjoy sex is a slut, but a man is merely a Casanova, a Don Juan, a playboy, a stud. All rather jolly sounding terms. Compare them with the word *slut*. Is it possible to get more contempt into four letters than into the sound of *slut*?

Listen to the moral outrage society expresses in its language, so rich in pejoratives for the woman who is not chaste: jade, whore, strumpet, harlot, bawd, wench, drab, bitch, streetwalker, baggage, chippy, madam, harridan, erring sister, tramp. How many of those terms suggest prostitution—the implication being that if a woman is not "pure" she *must* be selling it. (Men can't afford to acknowledge that women might indulge in sex for the same reason they do.)

The most common names a man is called in anger refer not to qualities about himself, but to his mother's chastity: "bastard" (his mother wasn't properly married) or "son of a bitch" (his mother is as promiscuous as a female dog in heat). The newer epithet "mother-fucker" represents a little progress in that it refers to the *behavior* of the man, not just his mother's lack of chastity, but even in this his mother is involved in an abominable act. The father, one notices, is never mentioned; his person and activities are not vulnerable to reproach.

It is against this matrix of highly charged emotions with respect to a woman's chastity, which has no corresponding concern regarding the male's sexual habits, that the crime of rape is judged. There is no middle ground for society's feelings about a woman's sexuality. If the woman is chaste, then her loss of purity is to be savagely avenged; only the ultimate punishment seems suitable for the ultimate outrage. If she is not unimpeachably chaste, then the law, which is to serve only those approved by society, does not apply; the woman only got what she deserved. Medieval though it be, the attitude persists; the crime is still judged today against the rankest of double standards.

Rape was made a felony under the Old English common law on which American jurisprudence is based. Most of the code dealing with sexuality in the United States has not been revised for one hundred years. It varies widely from state to state. What is punishable by fifteen years in prison in one state is acceptable in another if the victim is more than ten years of age. Inequalities in definitions of crimes are bad and inequalities in sentencing are even worse. In California one judge sentenced a rape offender to fifty-two weekends in jail; in North Carolina the death penalty is mandatory.

The law traditionally lags in reflecting needed changes in a social system; still it is time, and more, to consider why a woman's asking for legal justice in a case of rape amounts to a second victimization.

The Victim Before the Law

Losers are not popular in a competitive society. No one admires them or cares to identify with them. It is assumed that their position is somehow what they deserve. The opprobrium extends even to *blaming* a victim for his misfortune; if the person were different it would not have occurred. A rationale may even be developed to explain why the victim *merits* victimization. A case in point: after the murder of the four Kent State students, a rumor was circulated, and apparently believed by townspeople eager to neutralize the guilt, that the two girls were pregnant. This implied that (1) they were "unworthy," acceptable victims, and (2) their actions were probably suicidal; they had shameful reasons for provoking the shooting. Again one notes the usefulness of a claim of unchastity for wrecking the image of a female.

The rape victim quickly learns the low status of a loser, and particularly one in a sexual context, when she turns to society for justice and often finds the law and its representatives as pitiless as the man who raped her. She has to deal with police who are often so calloused that only a rare element of violence or spice rouses their interest; the medical treatment given her is often far inferior to what it might be, and worst of all, she encounters a legal system designed to protect her offender so that it is she and not he who is on trial.

To be mistreated where one looks for aid and comfort seems a monstrous betrayal; the shock is often worse than that of the original crime in which the victim had no prior expectations, felt no moral claims. The rude lesson begins with her first questioning. If she does not report the attack within an hour the police may suspiciously scold: "Why didn't you call at once? What have you been doing since then?" as if the only reason for not functioning properly after a rape were lack of civic responsibility. She will have to tell her story first to the officer who answers her call, then in such detail that it sometimes requires several hours, to the inspector who prepares her case for the district attorney. The techniques of law enforcement agencies that have not responded to feminist pressures for better treatment of victims can be crude. The questions can be inane ("What was he doing with his left hand?"), voyeuristic ("Did he have a big cock?"), cynical ("Are you sure you didn't smile at him?"), censorious ("Were you wearing a bra?"), or derisive ("Why didn't you keep your legs together?"). Some of the more important ones, like "In which direction did he leave?" or "Do you have anything that might have his fingerprints?" often get overlooked in a fine-tooth combing of the erotic elements.

From the police station the victim is taken to a hospital or clinic for corroborating examination and treatment. Many doctors, it appears, have their own theories and fantasies, mostly medieval, about rape, and this shows in their dealings with rape victims. Women complain of rudely laconic answers to questions about venereal disease and pregnancy, of contemptuous indifference to bruises and hurts that are not yet visible. A speculum rammed into a vagina already scraped raw with sand is agonizing. Often a woman is not advised about the morning-after pill, or, if it is offered, the side effects are not explained. She may not learn that it will be two to three weeks before she is sure she does not have gonorrhea, six to eight weeks for syphilis.

If she decides to prosecute, she will be required to sign papers, submit to photographs of injuries, examine the mug book, point out the offender in a lineup, tell her story again to the district attorney who tries to prepare her for the stiff cross-examination the defense is sure to make, and finally face the preliminary hearing. Several weeks may have elapsed. If she was seriously injured, it may have been longer. During this time the victim often finds that the criminal injury was only the first loss; she experiences additional losses as those who are close to her feel guilt, embarrassment, and a loss of status by association, particularly if the offender was from a lower social group. Instead of the unquestioning sympathy and support the woman had hoped for, she may encounter a variety of behavior that only increases her sense of isolation and unhappiness. The event becomes a sort of springboard for the aggravation of the psychological quirks of everyone around her. The man in her life may act suspicious, injured, or even patronizing ("I'm not going to let this change our relationship"). Friends may turn cynical and distant, fearful of being involved, or, on the contrary, evidence a greedy satisfaction in the drama. Parents become angry, vindictive ("How many times have I told you . . .").

There may be additional psychological fallout if the story appears in the newspapers: snide remarks from neighborhood contacts or attentions from barely known males trying to cash in on the event. One victim was hounded by photographers during the weeks between the arraignment and the preliminary hearing. Hired by the offender, they were trying to get pictures of her with a number of men, in order to prove her morally loose.

Setting the legal machinery in motion can have unforeseen results: all persons reporting to a police station are automatically checked for outstanding warrants. Several unpaid traffic citations were dug up against one victim; she was reprimanded for them and released, and heard nothing more about her case. Women who have been abducted from one county to another have had their cases submerged in a snarl of jurisdictional problems.

The victim may be surprised to have the defense counsel for the case, in a wily move, contact her before she has spoken with her own counsel. Using glib excuses, not to say outright lies, the defense may pretend he has been unable to get a report of the case from the district attorney's office, so he must talk to her to get the facts. In this maneuver he hopes to get statements which, removed from context, can be used against her, as will the testimony of neighbors or anyone else who can be questioned about the matter. Meanwhile the victim usually has no contact with the legal counsel who is supposed to be her ally until the day of the hearing, sometimes only an hour before she faces the court. He is not supposed to give her any legal advice; he is not even supposed to warn her that she should not talk to the defense when they make overtures to her. Often the hearing is scheduled for nine in the morning, and the woman meets her lawyer for the first time at eight o'clock. That she may be clammy with fright, that she has no idea of what to expect in court, that she might like the simple comfort of seeing the face of the person who is going to represent her, or that she might have new facts or additional details to communicate since she gave her story to the police inspector—all this often seems to be of no interest to the D.A.'s office, even though its record for success will depend on her performance as a witness.

The victim who agrees to prosecute at the time of reporting to the police may, when she realizes how callous the official process is, regret her decision, particularly if she does not have an advocate from a rape-crisis group to guide and support her through the process. She may opt to withdraw, with a *nolle prosequi*, but if the state is determined to prosecute, it may do so, calling her as a witness with a subpoena. Willy nilly, she may have to face the accused and testify.

Whatever the pressures and humiliation she has been through before the preliminary hearing, they are only a prelude to what is in store for her when she faces a court made up almost entirely of men, white, middle-aged, and severely middle-class in demeanor and point of view, the "straights" of society.

The business of the district attorney, the prosecution, is to establish that a rape took place and that it was the accused who did it. The business of the defense attorney is to refute, by one of several means, that his client is guilty of rape. Unless the evidence is incontrovertible or the offender has confessed, the defense attorney may try to prove that it was not his client. Or, he may admit that sexual intercourse took place between the accused and the accuser, but claim that the woman consented. He may go further and claim that she provoked the situation by teasing and inviting, and that the accused only acted out of "normal instincts." Or he may even claim that the woman was so aggressive that the man was obliged to defend himself by pushing or hitting her, so she, in the fury of a scorned woman, is claiming rape. Often he tries to disprove the woman's veracity. If he can catch her in one error of memory or falsehood he will use it to show that her word cannot be trusted. Finally, the defense may try to neutralize the guilt of the offender by proving that the woman, because of a bad reputation, cannot claim the privileges of a victim before the law.

The offender's defense, then, besides mistaken identity, is one (or more) of these: the woman lied, the woman consented, the woman provoked, the woman is not worthy of the law's protection. It is the woman, not the offender, who is on the defensive.

The peculiar nature of a rape hearing is due to the fact that the crime is so easy for a woman to claim and so hard for a man to disprove. Without witnesses or evidence of brutality, common when a victim yields to avoid being hurt, the trial depends solely on the testimony of the plaintiff. Unseen and unheard, the crime often leaves no trace except in the mind of the victim. A man's fate, ranging from a few months of imprisonment to a penalty of death, may depend on the exactness of the woman's word.

The unfounded rape claim is as old as history; in the first book of the Bible, Pharaoh's captain, Potiphar, had a wife who tried to seduce Joseph and, failing, claimed rape (Genesis 39:7–20).

The devices of vengeful women to substantiate their claims to rape can be imaginative. They have torn their clothes to simulate violence, scratched their own faces, beaten themselves with strange objects. A claim of rape is the easiest kind of serious trouble that an unscrupulous woman can lay on a man. Why would she resort to such an accusation? Like Potiphar's wife, to punish a man she secretly desires. Or to conceal her own misconduct. In the South, a white woman might have sexual relations willingly with a black man, then fear pregnancy, panic, and claim rape. Only a few years ago, the accused man could be lynched. If a white woman were discovered to have had sexual relations with a black and she did not claim it was rape, she could be lynched herself.

Besides easing her conscience about a sexual adventure or camouflaging her own acts, a woman's reason for falsely claiming rape might be that the man she had relations with did not meet her expectations romantically. She might have wanted him to buy her a present, offer a trip, proclaim his love. If she finds him stingy or bad-tempered or indifferent she cannot punish him legally for these things, but she can make a lot of trouble if she claims rape.

Occasionally a woman makes a claim of rape, later proved unfounded, that is not directed at a specific offender. This can be a delayed working out of an earlier trauma in her life. An investigation of the woman's past may show that although she was not raped recently, as she claimed, she had in fact been raped or sexually abused earlier, often as a young teen-ager. It is as if this material that had never been revealed remained psychologically unassimilated and returned in another form, later. This may occur when a woman is going through a crisis like divorce, or some other event where she feels hurt, abused. However misplaced, it is a cry for help; the woman has mistakenly turned to the law instead of to mental health resources.

The veracity of most victims, however, is beyond doubt. In the numerous questionings she must endure before appearing in court her sincerity is severely tested; the snags in a fraudulent claim have little chance of escaping the trained, not to say cynical, eyes of the many persons involved in processing her claim.

If there is no evident brutality in the case the defense attorney usually tries to show that the plaintiff consented. How is consent proved when it is one person's word against the other's and the accuser has little to lose legally while the accused has a great deal to lose? Defense attorneys have resorted to ~~appallingly~~ sly and damaging tactics against the victim. One of the oldest is the now discredited Sancho Panza ploy of proving that it is impossible to rape an unwilling victim: a witness is asked to try to put his finger in the mouth of a bottle which is being moved about briskly in front of him.

If the victim and the offender had a friendly or close relationship before the event, the case has little chance of succeeding in court. Even if there is considerable evidence of brutality—if the woman was slammed against the refrigerator so hard that she broke three hair curlers and passed out—a court may be reluctant to intervene in what it will assume is a lover's quarrel trumped up into something more. Rape by someone you know, ~~goes the official attitude,~~ is a form of love. The law assumes a continued state of mind. If the woman has dated the man or been to bed with him before, ~~balking at the time of the event, the court implies,~~ is at her own peril; it is not the business of the law to intervene in such matters.

If the victim did not previously know the offender, the most common method of trying to establish consent in the event is to show that the woman elsewhere consented to sexual relations outside a marital context. If this can be proved then ~~it is implied that~~ she is "the consenting sort" and consented here. The defense thus becomes a headlong attack on the woman's character. Besides being made out as an accomplice, not a victim, in the case, she is made to seem an unworthy witness. Having a lover or having relations with a number of men is used to suggest that her sexual availability outside the law puts *her* outside the law's protection. In effect then, the law does not protect anyone who does not adhere to the strictest legal standards (one hundred years old) about sexual matters.

There is also an invidious taint of general untrustworthiness, as if making love outside approved legal arrangements establishes other doubts about her character, such as her honesty. If she isn't chaste, she must be a liar too.

Because it is as hard to disprove rape as it is to prove it, the law has traditionally demanded that the victim show she used "utmost resistance" in defending herself. Physical evidence of brutality is one of the criteria of an authentic case. Ironically, the woman attacked by an armed man may have less evidence of brutality to show than one subdued by an offender who used no weapon but beat her with his fists. The more serious threat may reduce the victim to submission instantly, without a scratch. Thus, with a knife, gun, or piece of rope the offender can eliminate the evidence against himself. (If the crime is prosecuted, the charge of armed assault is more serious, but offenders are rarely concerned with such considerations. They act out what pleases them.) It is possible too, that a woman will have no chance to resist; she may be seized from behind, her hands tied with her scarf, and because the offender is far stronger than herself, no further violence is necessary. She may have only chafed wrists and vague body aches to show for the experience.

If the defense cannot prove that the plaintiff consented, tacitly, by lack of resistance, he can try to mitigate the charges by showing that the act was "victim-precipitated." That the woman by provocative behavior produced a situation in which the man's response was "normal," not criminal. Inviting a man to one's apartment after a show is considered a clear signal; leaving a bar with a man whom one has met there, or hitchhiking, is even worse. Refusing to have sex then is considered an unfair reversal of signals. The assumption is that consent has been given in advance; the man thus has the *right* to insist. The thinking here is circular. By putting herself in a vulnerable situation a woman arouses man's desire, and his desire gives him the right. (If the desire imperative is absolute, how strange that the woman's negative desire has so little consideration.)

If a woman smiles at a man, talks to him, or in any way shows an interest in him, or if he *thinks* she is showing an interest in him, this may be construed as provocative behavior. "Every time I looked at her she recrossed her legs." It may be all in his head, especially if he has been drinking, but if he thinks he has received signals, his behavior will be explained as justified. Another twist of male chauvinist logic is involved here. If a woman is (or seems) provocative and then fails to live up to her come-on, she should be punished. How? By the man's brutally taking what she seemed to have promised in the first place. "Right by punishment" of a tease is an example of the deserving principle. The victim got what she deserved. Since almost anything a woman does can be construed, by a mind determined to do so, as provocative, the offender's imagination is all that is necessary to make a rape victim-precipitated. In *The Diary of a Rapist*, the sick, warped writer was convinced that the winner of a beauty pageant had picked him out of the huge crowd at the event and had given him the looks and signals that led to his just and inevitable act later.

Finally, in the curious balancing scale of this crime, in which lowering the reputation of one protagonist raises the reputation of the other, defense counsel will use every means to expose "moral weakness" in the victim. To do this the court will listen to an exhaustive inquiry into her character.

Who *is* she? What is her reputation? Is she known to drink? To go to bars? Has she ever been on welfare (implying a need to prostitute herself)? How long has she held her job? Does she own a car (or does she hitchhike)? Does she date many men? How many? What kind? Is she a divorcée? Does she take part in demonstrations for abortion, express unpopular opinions? Does she have nude art on her walls, does she sunbathe on her fire escape, wear a bikini to the market in summer? Do people with different colored skins appear at her parties? Has she ever used "grass," lived in a commune, been to Cuba?

By proving that a victim is given to behavior that the straight society sees as odd or untrustworthy, the defense establishes a moral field for the shaft "How many men have you slept with in your life?" or "When do you have intercourse?"

Except under special circumstances, at his counsel's choice, the offender is never put on the witness stand where he could be cross-examined. His veracity is not in question. Whether he plasters his walls with nude pinups, answers the door in his underwear, or consorts with call girls is of no interest to the court. His character is not at stake, only his behavior in this one event. He may have a police record of a dozen rapes against him, but these cannot be admitted as evidence. Only if he has had prior convictions for rape can these, by special legal maneuvering, be admitted as a form of "course of action" of the accused.

Because the case becomes a contest of credibility the defense works constantly to prove that the woman cannot be believed. In cunningly phrased questions he will try to confuse her into contradicting herself. If he can catch her in a single mistake of name, time, or place on any subject he will submit this as evidence of her unreliability. If he can prove that she lied to her boss just once when she called in sick, her veracity will be disavowed, her case will begin to crumble.

Another tactic will be to prove that she hates men, and this one in particular, and that her motives in claiming rape are vengeful. He may ask her diabolically unanswerable questions, the equivalent of "Have you stopped beating your wife?" in order to excite her into a display of anger and hostility before the court.

The patent unfairness of the trial proceedings, their bias in favor of the offender, reaches a climax in the judge's instructions to the jury. In no other case is the jury warned against the testimony of the plaintiff. The last words the jurors hear as they leave the chambers to decide the verdict is the judge's reminder that "rape is easy to claim, hard to prove."

13

The Law: An Instrument for New Justice

The problem of rape is clearly not going to diminish until the laws pertaining to it are reformed. As long as women are intimidated by the law, as long as chances for justice seem poor if not hopeless, there is no real reason, outside an exceptional sense of civic duty, that a woman should extend her humiliation by reporting it. And as long as the crime is underreported it cannot be properly understood nor the proper measures taken against it.

In most states the victim receives no compensation for the damages she has suffered. She may need medical care, her clothes may have to be replaced, she may see a psychiatrist for months afterward in order to get over trembling when she hears a car stop in her street, late at night. She may lose time at work because of hospitalization and legal duties. A few of the more enlightened communities now give free medical treatment, paid for by the county, to all victims reporting to the police. This includes a pelvic examination, treatment against V.D. and pregnancy, and emergency treatment for contusions, breaks, and lacerations. However, nowhere in the United States is there anything like the system in Sweden, where the victim can receive an indemnity from her convicted offender. The pay he accrues while working in the penal system is applied to reimbursing her expenses, including psychiatric services. There is a satisfying relationship in this direct responsibility to the victim; it also establishes a connection between the severity of the woman's suffering and the man's sentence. The man who does not see what he did as a crime against society can count the days it takes him to work off the price of replacing an old woman's broken dental plates. The hours he puts in at hard labor are far more real than a sentence based on such irrelevant factors as how much desire for exemplary punishment the case has produced. And the woman is encouraged to report in this system which acknowledges the debt of the offender to his victim.

In the chain of legal processes today, perhaps only one rape case in a hundred survives from commission through reporting, arrest, prosecution, conviction, and incarceration. As long as the man who rapes knows that he has a 99 percent chance of remaining free to continue, rape will continue to rise. Every unreported, unprosecuted rape only adds to the confidence of the offenders and thus to the pool of potential pain and violence awaiting other victims.

Each year the figures grow larger, both in totals and in per capita crime rates. The pressures that create the crime continue to rise, and aside from sporadic promises from politicians of safer streets, very little if anything is being done to get at the roots and causes of rape.

One of the first steps must be to change the existing laws, which are unfair to both men and women. When penalties are too harsh, victims have little chance of winning a prosecution. Ironically, the more astringent laws are in dealing with a convicted rape offender, the less chance a victim has to win her plaint. Reducing the existing penalties of death or life imprisonment would encourage prosecutors to accept cases that are more complex, and in which there is less evidence of brutality, even if it is no less real. Victims with a better chance of convicting would be encouraged to go through the misery of prosecuting. The monstrousness of some aspects of the crime by Victorian standards has been palliated by the freer sexual tempo of the day. The existing laws, which are hopelessly out of date, should be rewritten for the sake of everyone involved.

One of the most unfair elements in the legal process is the defense's right to cross-examine the victim about prior sex acts in order to establish whether she might have given consent. Where there is evidence of brutality, supported by police and medical testimony, this is clearly absurd. Jurists admit that the procedure amounts to an open hunting season on the victim's character. The real purpose of introducing the victim's sexual history at the preliminary hearing is to intimidate her, in order to have more leverage for the plea bargaining that the defense often negotiates to avoid a superior court hearing. It is a cynical maneuver, designed not really to prove that she might have consented, but to frighten the victim so she will be reluctant to testify again in the higher court. Since the defendant's previous history cannot be revealed, the plaintiff's should not be either.

The American Civil Liberties Union has fought attempts to revise the law on admission of previous sexual history on the curious theory that it would establish a precedent for not allowing a victim's background to be shown in an assault case. In assault, the reasoning goes, the plaintiff might be shown by past acts to be of a quarrelsome, provoking nature which, in effect, produced assaults. Rapecrisis groups dismiss this reasoning as specious: it is equating sex with assault when they are not at all the same. Assault is always an illegal activity. Sex is not.

The judge's cautionary instructions to the jury before they leave to deliberate is a unique event in law procedures. It is mandatory in all rape cases, but many jurors do not know this and assume that the judge is warning them that he personally does not believe the case to be authentic and is asking for a verdict of "not guilty." The warning was made mandatory in the days when death was commonly the penalty of rape, and a man's life was at stake. Sentences today are more likely to range from two to ten years in prison, but the cautionary instruction has remained. Why, it is time to ask, should this be necessary if it is unneeded in any other legal proceeding?

Another court rule that operates against the victim is that the defense can have the preliminary hearing closed to the public, in order to protect the reputation of the accused in case charges cannot be proved. However, there is no equal protection for the victim; the prosecution cannot ask for a closed hearing; the public may listen to detailed questioning about her sexual past. Friends of the defendant may be present in the court, giving her looks threatening revenge while she recites her story, and the first answer she must give under oath is her correct address.

Since rape is considered a crime against the state, only the state can prosecute. If a defense attorney is not convinced of a victim's story (or does not think the case can be won—which would go against his win record), he can refuse the case, and since she cannot move it to another county or have it heard by hiring a private lawyer, there is no way she can obtain justice. If a district attorney is a male chauvinist who dislikes women on the one hand and doesn't think that forcing a women sexually is really a crime on the other, a county can acquire an astonishingly clean record for nonrape.

Finally, in a rape hearing, the defendant never takes the stand; he is not required to answer even the simplest questions about the case or himself, while the victim may be cross-examined at length. She may be held in the witness chair for hours, harassed by questions that are both loaded and sarcastic and that are clearly intended to wear her down until she can no longer give a creditable account. The defense's case, quite simply, is built on the destruction of the victim's story. The accused takes the stand only if his attorney is convinced that his client's past and demeanor are so impeccable that they can only be favorable to the case. But, film accounts to the contrary, this is extremely rare.

Often in a rape trial it is not the facts of the event that are judged so much as a series of legal maneuvers. As one victim sadly recounted afterwards, "With what gets blown out of proportion, and what is misrepresented, and what they don't let you say that *is* true, the case sounds so different from what really happened you hardly recognize it as your own."

In sentencing, also, the rape offender's punishment does not depend upon the facts of the case as much as upon his luck in choosing a legally vulnerable victim. What he has done to her really does not matter: he may have seized her with great violence, menaced her with a gun or knife, forced her into sodomy or oral coitus, threatened her repeatedly with death, injected drugs into her body, abducted her and tormented her for days. But if she had an abortion as a juvenile, or if she lives in a sexually free hippy commune, or has anything else in her past or life-style that makes her a vulnerable witness, the case may never be heard, or if heard may be reduced, through plea bargaining, to one or two of the least serious charges. For committing ten heinous crimes an offender may plead guilty to two of the lesser counts and be sentenced to as little as four years. In one such case, an offender was freed, having had no therapy or noticeable rehabilitation, after serving eighteen months for burglary. Within twenty-four hours he was picked up on a new charge of oral copulation with a child of eight.

What kind of justice have we when the penalty for a crime depends not on the acts of the offender but on the past of the victim? This is the most grotesque kind of double-standard blackmail. The law, in itself, is a crime against women.

Whatever the sentence given to the offender, it is likely to have little meaning in terms of desired effects. Prison terms are no deterrent to the crime of rape. Time in jail only turns out to be an education in sexual aberrations, besides reinforcing hostility and antisocial behavior. Theoretically, imprisonment has a threefold purpose: to rehabilitate the offender, by example to deter others from the crime, and to protect society from the offender.

The first two of these purposes generally are not served at all. Rehabilitation in most penal systems is at a minimum and the man who rapes is not deterred by the fate of others; even the death penalty is no terror bar to one whose antisocial impulses reach a suicidal pitch. Society may be protected for a while by the imprisonment of an offender, but if when he is released he is more angry and cunning than ever, with connections in the underworld that take him into such noxious activities as drugs and homicide, society is not really ahead.

The problem is particularly difficult in the case of the youth whose rape is an acting-out of a pattern of violence that is not uncommon in his subculture. When he is between seventeen and twenty-five he may carry out antisocial acts considered normal among his peers. Past that age he tends to give up this kind of activity of his own accord. If he is put in prison or reform school during those years, some rapes may be prevented, but the toll in hardened attitudes together with a new criminal know-how is no real gain.

The punishment should fit the offender, not the crime. Recognition of different kinds of offenders should create more meaningful forms of justice. The ghetto boy who rapes his cousin because everyone else in his gang has raped *someone* is quite different from the psychopath who seizes women at lonely bus stops; and the man who thinks a coerced seduction is the way you treat a date is still another sort. Sentencing is an important topic in a discussion of prevention of the crime because offenders are often repeaters, and because, as has been pointed out, too harsh penalties prevent prosecution.

Some of the states have made advances in improving sentencing procedures that could well be emulated by others. Wisconsin has a remarkably good Sex Crimes Law, which, it should be noted, was drawn up by its citizens. A man convicted of a sex offense is not given to the penal authorities but bound over to the department of public welfare, where he is examined by experts and held for rehabilitation until all are agreed that he is ready to adjust to society. Massachusetts and, until recently, California, had good treatment facilities. In California, the ill-conceived attempt to empty hospitals for the criminally insane and return patients to their communities has produced a disastrous trail of bloody crimes.

Indeterminate sentencing, which at one time seemed humane and sensible, the offender being kept in jail for as long or as short a time as was necessary for his rehabilitation, has proved a booby trap of abuse. Offenders detest such a sentence because they fear that sentences are extended out of personal antipathies; society on the other hand fears that troublemakers are released too early, just to get rid of them. Most offenders would prefer a concrete term of a stipulated number of years.

Federal Judge Marvin Frankel's proposal that a judge should confer with two colleagues on each sentence has merit. As Frankel points out in his book *Criminal Sentences: Law Without Order,* judges spend days hearing the points in a case and studying its legal technicalities, but rarely give much time—often no more than an hour—to deciding a man's sentence. Since judges cannot make up the laws for themselves on other questions they should not be allowed sweeping powers here. The extreme differences sometimes found between sentences in similar cases makes a mockery of the whole legal process. The law cannot hold the respect of either the offender or the victim until a method of consistency and impartiality guarantees the rights of all who come before it.

Rape sentences today usually do not show concern for the most important consideration in the crime: why men rape, why this particular offender committed rape. Until the motivations for this curious, unprofitable crime are dealt with, neither the offender at hand nor others will be deterred. Those who go through the jail terms and superficial psychological screening presently offered are no more cured than a cancer victim after one visit to a doctor. The cleverer ones actually profit from the contact by acquiring a vocabulary of excuses. They pick up jargon like "ghetto background," "broken family," and "peer-group rivalry" and cynically use it on their probation officer the next time around.

Sentencing should be derived from a consideration of many factors, with scales for determining not only the seriousness of the crime to society but the personal responsibility of this particular offender. Such scales might include the following considerations:

Gravity of the Crime

1. Amount of brutality and humiliation
2. Number of offenses in the crime (abduction, sodomy, etc.)
3. Whether or not planned (a) the encounter, (b) the violence
4. Weapon used?
5. Amount of violence threatened, or other threat
6. Prior contact or relationship with victim
7. Alcohol present (in victim or offender)?
8. Place, time, situation
9. Age of victim; difference in age with offender
10. Opportunity to escape not used by victim?
11. Precipitating circumstances of incident

Responsibility of the Offender
(for determining disposition of case)

1. Age
2. Background—economic and social
3. Schooling
4. Employment record
5. Family history
6. Marital status
7. Resources (friends, finances, job training)
8. Explanation of event given by offender
9. Prior offenses (a) of the same nature, (b) of a different nature
10. Offender's legal position: plea
11. Relationship with other offender in crime, if any
12. Medical history

In studying the scales it becomes clear that a nineteen-year-old unemployed black with a fourth-grade education and no father, whose uptight, superreligious mother has, after a quarrel, kicked him out of her home, should not be judged by the same standards nor receive the same kind of sentence as a white, middle-aged used-car salesman, twice divorced, who rapes a girl he picks up at a newsstand during an out-of-town convention. The fact that for either man the victim might be a barefoot hippy who lives precariously by selling, off a New York sidewalk, evil-eye beads on leather thongs should have nothing to do with the trial procedure or the punishment of either offender.

Judges, with good-hearted earnestness, sometimes pass out advice that is so wide of the mark it would be hilarious if the implications were not so grave. One suggested that the defendant, when he had completed his six-month jail term, "take some wilderness trips." Somehow, it had not occurred to the judge that the young Italian before him who had been put in an orphanage at the age of eight and had been in and out of mental institutions and reform schools ever since, and who even acknowledged that "his head was sometimes twitchy," was in desperate need of psychotherapy. The principal consideration in the disposition of the case, an attempted rape of a thirteen-year-old girl, was the fact that the girl had not actually been penetrated. She had suffered only the inconvenience of the assault, the police questioning, and finally the court hearing, and this mitigated the gravity of the crime. The fact that the highly nervous young offender, who had had no home for seventeen years and who hadn't even a present address, might next time take an axe to accomplish the deed was not considered.

In this case also, the offender's sentence was not based on the gravity of his crime but on the vulnerability of the young victim. In order to spare her another hearing, the next time in an open court, the prosecution agreed to let the defense plead guilty to a lesser charge of simple assault.

Clearly, there must be a new legal approach to the crime. New solutions must be worked out that consider both the needs of the victim and the rights of the accused. A recognition of the complexity of the crime might begin with its reclassification.

Much of the legal confusion surrounding the crime of rape has arisen from attempts to judge it against a single set of criteria, instead of recognizing the highly differing circumstances under which it may occur. Clearly, the case of a woman who has for several years had a casual, neighborly relation with the man who raped her cannot be judged against the same criteria as a woman attacked by a stranger in a Safeway parking lot. Establishing different categories based on the relationship, or lack of it, between the persons involved would make it possible to judge these differing cases with more fairness to both victims and offenders. Eliminating the inflammatory word "rape" altogether in the legal process might be useful. The following groups suggest themselves.

Sexual assault by a stranger (1st degree). This is the most serious and clear-cut case of criminal aggression.

Sexual assault by an offender known to a victim (2nd degree). While this can be no less serious than the first-degree crime in its traumatic effects, because of the previous relationship it is more complex and involves special considerations.

Sexual assault by a new acquaintance (3rd degree). In this case the victim shares the responsibility for initiating the situation that led to the rape, as in hitchhiking.

The most difficult case to prosecute has traditionally been that of the offender who has been the working colleague, friend, ex-lover, or date of the victim, and yet these cases can be as violent and painful as any other. District attorneys have been known to refuse to process such cases, no matter how battered the victim, on the craven excuse that a jury would not convict so there was no use trying.

Because of the old myths that surround the rapist as sex fiend or archcriminal it is hard to cast a close friend or neighbor as an offender. One can imagine a stranger as a shadowy and menacing personage, filthy, violent, possibly diseased. Outrage against a stranger is easy. But one's friends and neighbors are expected to be like one's self, clean, kindly, responsible. They do not fit the rape stereotype, it is hard to imagine the Jekyll and Hyde change that claiming rape by a known offender involves. (Implied also: What happened to make that change? What did the victim do to precipitate a change?)

It is time for both the public and the law to be disabused of some of the satisfyingly simplistic images that have reigned for years. According to Amir's study 30.6 percent of the victims knew the offender well: 19.3 percent were close neighbors, 6 percent were close friends or boyfriends, and 5.3 percent were friends of the family. If one adds the 2.5 percent who were male relatives, more than one third of the group were men who violated positions of friendship and trust. Given the general reluctance of the victim to prosecute in such cases, the total of 214 probably represents at least ten times as many, more than 2,000 cases. Other studies have produced similar results.

The victim who prosecutes someone she knows well does so from a very different emotional set than the victim who prosecutes a stranger. The law should regard her claim with quite different criteria. She deserves special treatment for these reasons:

1. She must be especially strongly motivated in order to overcome the feelings, positive or neutral, that she had for the man before he became her offender. This is important for both the district attorney and the defense, who must watch for a fradulent claim. Is she acting out of vindictiveness or is it honest outrage?

2. She will have much stronger feelings of guilt and self-reproach than with a stranger-offender.

3. She may fear retribution from the offender or his friends, who know where she lives, her activities, and the members of her family. Not only she but they become vulnerable.

4. It involves people who are known to both victim and offender, and these parents, relatives, in-laws, and friends become secondary victims in a rape trial, suffering guilt, humiliation, and loss of status, making it harder for the victim to prosecute.

5. Because the case is not simple and clear cut, chances of pain and aggravation during the trial are increased, chances of success decreased.

6. Rape by an offender who is known to the victim produces a loss of trust toward those whom she should be able to trust. And the girl or woman who loses this trust in males, in friends, has lost

something essential to her personality, perhaps for life. "Trust, like the soul, once departed, never returns."

In sum, then, while the psychic damage to the victim of a stranger attack is fear, establishing a long-lasting sense apprehension and anxiety, the psychic damage to the victim who knows her offender is loss of trust. The difference between this fear and loss of trust is well illustrated in the case of Jane, as she shall be known here. While Jane and a woman friend were hitchhiking they were joined by a young man with whom they became friendly, Larry. A van passed them, then returned and picked them up. The driver, John, a Vietnam veteran, soon left the freeway, produced a gun, and forced the three of them through many sexual acts. It was winter and the young women were naked for several hours. Jane said later, "I knew I was cold but I was so terrified it seemed unimportant. Dying or living, that was the thing, and it looked close. But what shocked me most, after all that we were forced to do, was when Larry, on his own initiative, put his hand on my breast. I couldn't believe it, after we'd taken him for our friend. I whispered to him to take it away. He did, but then he put it back again. The rest was terror but that was betrayal. That *hurt*. Two years later it still hurts. I don't trust men now."

Sexual assault by the new acquaintance, because it involves a precipitating action by the victim, is responsible for much of the judgmental attitude that male chauvinists apply to the rape victim. By entering a vulnerable situation of her own free will a woman may be guilty of failing to protect herself, but this is not a crime and does not give license for a criminal attack. In such situations the victim errs at two critical turning points, when she could avoid the crime. The first mistake is her initial move, as when she puts out her thumb on a road, or enters a bar alone. The second is during the interaction with the man who becomes the offender. In the bar she could refuse to talk to him, or to leave with him; on the road she could decline the ride. Often there is a third turning point before it is too irrevocably late: when the man gives a signal, when he communicates what is on his mind by something he says or does. This kind of crime might be described as "avoidable rape."

It does not take much brains for a woman to know that she cannot freely go anywhere at any time with any man. While this may not be fair, and may in fact be one of the things that most needs correcting in our society, we are not yet at the point where women can act with freedom, and the problem must be dealt with step by step. When the millenium comes perhaps everyone will have the right to expect kind and decent treatment from everyone else, but in the meantime no amount of shouting about the right to be safe while hitchhiking is going to make it safe. Feminists may claim that to acknowledge this danger is to accept its right to exist, a cop-out. I say that not to recognize reality while working to change it is not really useful if, in defiance, women are needlessly hurt.

It should be made clear that there is no moral judgment implied against the victim who enters a vulnerable situation or fails to heed signals. It is not a matter of being provocative, nor does it reflect on her reputation or sexuality any more than being drawn into a swindle in which the victim pays for naiveté. However, a victim who by obstinacy in the first issue and heedlessness in the second does not protect herself is not in a position that is as legally impeccable as one who is attacked without warning by a stranger. Still, like the corpse that knows no difference between first- and second-degree murder, the sufferings of a victim of sexual assault are just as real whether she has been remiss in her responsibilities to herself or not.

In the case of Jane and the other hitchhikers abducted and assaulted at gunpoint by the Vietnam veteran, the three critical turning points or choices had been evident but ignored; the victims had felt safe in their number. They *chose* to hitchhike, they *chose* to ride with that driver, although he had passed them and returned to pick them up, which is considered a warning sign, and they also did not heed or react to two other distinct signals: the man's exploratory talk about nudist camps and then his announcement that he was going to make a detour off the freeway.

A large number of authentic rape cases are refused each year by district attorneys' offices on the excuse that no jury would convict an offender who is known to his victim. The court's calendar is crowded, they say, and rape cases can be long and costly; it is a waste of the court's time to try a case that is not likely to win. The real reason is hardly so disinterested. Since each attorney's professional advancement depends on his win-lose record, why should he take a case that will not add a feather to his cap? "They're waiting for the perfect rape case," commented one bitter rape-crisis-center advocate, after still another battered victim was told she hadn't a ghost of a chance of getting a conviction, because the offender was a former boyfriend.

Is it morally acceptable for servants of the state to view rape victims only in terms of their own personal advancement? Rape-crisis groups take a strong position here. The victim who knows her offender can no longer be dismissed as an unfeasible plaintiff. She represents an enormous segment of pain and abuse; the crime against her is the least reported and least prosecuted of all violent crimes. District attorneys' offices are going to have to be more responsive to the needs of the people they are supposed to serve. And an enlightened citizenry, serving as jurors, must be educated to elements more complex than those of the old myths. If the crime of rape is reclassified, legally, to acknowledge the subtleties of different kinds of circumstances and allow these different degrees of criminal action to be judged on separate criteria, an important step toward justice will be made.

Society's attempts to deal with the crime of rape have for centuries been hedged about with vicious prejudices and superstitious nonsense. Perhaps most damaging among these has been the legend of chastity that has denied women equal sexual rights before the law. Now the pill is revolutionizing sexual attitudes; never again will they be the same. Amir's statistical studies have given the lie to many old simplistic myths about rape. Clearly, society is on the threshold of a new era in dealing with the crime. Reform of the legal process is urgent, true, but a correct handling of the murders and victims after the crime has been committed is not enough. Its causes must be understood, and action must be taken to eradicate the roots of the crime in those causes. How?

III

GROUP RAPE

14

Group Rape: A Special Kind

To be seized for rape by an overpowering stranger is one of the experiences most feared by many women. Only one thing seems worse: to be seized for rape by a group of men. Yet this event is more common than supposed. It accounts for one fourth of all the reported rapes in the United States. One half of all the men charged with this crime have taken part in a group rape.

Besides the trauma of its effect on the victim, the difference between rape by a single offender and rape by a group is profound, both in cause and purpose. This is of prime importance in working for the prevention of the crime as well as in determining punishment for the offender. The cause of rape by a single offender is to be found in the psychology of the individual. The cause of rape by a group is to be found in the sociology of the culture. Because group rape is a sociological phenomenon and does not lend itself to examination as easily as the case history of the single offender, it has received little attention in studies on the crime.

In group rape a single female is assaulted by three to thirty men in an event that, even if it lasts many hours and is interspersed with other activities such as drinking, fighting, and moving from place to place, still, by the peculiar psychology that prevails and unites the participants, is not a series of individual rapes but an act of the group. It is the group's perception of the event that is important, not the satisfaction of its members.

Group rape is a subcultural event. Members of a subculture live by values that are different from those of the dominating culture. In the delinquent subculture of the United States, sex is often not a private affair associated with feelings, and females are generally not treated as persons with sexual rights. Male members of the subculture have no real incentive to adopt the values of the majority, even if aware of them. On the contrary, they are under pressure to conform to the values of their own subculture.

Group rape, although frightful for the wretched victim and odious to the dominating culture, performs a function for the delinquent subculture that might be described as socializing. It is not a neurotic or aberrant activity, as is most rape by a single offender, but a means of fulfilling, for young male groups, certain needs and patterns that are common to all cultures. These include the need to share experiences with peers, the need to try out new roles as functioning sexual beings, and especially the need to be a part of a group, finding within its code and standards an identity above self.

The same human dynamics are at work in a delinquent subculture as in primitive tribes and Kiwanis clubs; group processes are the same everywhere. Leadership is provided by one who embodies the characteristics most prized by the group, and he is surrounded by an inner core of highly committed members and an outer ring of supporting fringe members. Relationships alter as members jockey for status and the group looks for tests to burnish its image and keep the membership in its thrall.

Why does a group turn to rape? The reasons often relate to problems within the membership. If interest is flagging and members are bored and restless, a dramatic event such as rape may seem a tonic means of providing adventure and status. Sometimes group rape is seized upon as a means of resolving a power crisis within the group. The leader may initiate the event to reassert his authority, or it may be a test organized by the inner core members to shake off or integrate fringe members into the group. Conversely, it may be initiated by fringe members trying to move into the core group or challenge its leadership.

Relations within groups that exist for the sole purpose of providing membership and identity are fragile; every project in which the members engage is loaded with potential in terms of shifts in the hierarchy of position. During a group rape, what the men do to the victim—their acts of brutality, the sex itself—is of less importance than what these acts achieve in establishing prestige within the group. Therefore, who strikes the first blow, who goes on the victim first, who is most violent, who plans the event or seduces the group by breaking down inhibitions—such acts and the bravado with which they are carried out become a means of determining rank.

As in most rape, the event is not based on the sexual needs of its members, many of whom have available sexual partners. It is not the sexual release but the fact that it takes place in the presence of the others, with their approval and complicity, that counts. The sharing of the act is more important than the act.

In this element group rape is different from all other crimes. When a group unites to commit a burglary, it is the stolen goods that are the object. Whatever esprit de corps develops during the operation, however useful to its success, is only a by-product. In group rape, it is the esprit de corps, above all, that matters.

Participating in a group rape may offer only limited satisfaction to the individual; to one who is frightened, disapproving, or sexually inexpert it may be a downright hardship. Conforming to the collective will of the group might almost be perceived as a symbolic sacrifice, the youths offering their masculinity to the group, which has need of such a sacrifice for the group's cohesiveness. This may be, in a young teen-ager's life, the first truly voluntary act of submission to an entity larger than self, the first use of instincts for loyalty, compromise, and magnanimity that are essential to human socialization.

For most of the participants, group rape is only a dramatic version of a not uncommon experience, group sex. The first sexual experience of a youth in a subcultural situation is often a collective one; older boys share a willing girl with him or a group of peers overcome their virginity in a group experience with a girl who is willing to show them how. Collective sex is a common feature of many subcultures, although usually limited to two or three performers at a time. It is a progression in male group behavior. The small boys gather to see who can pee the farthest; the young adolescents try group masturbation. In their middle teens they move on to sharing the same sexual object.

The principle remains the same: activity involving sexual organs is not a particularly private affair. It has little to do with females and even less with feelings. From such experiences, which appear as male acts, something *men* do, sometimes together, it is not a long step to heightening the event by using a female who must be subdued. From a male act the event is converted into the ultra-male act.

Group rape, it should be made clear, is not an orgy. Whereas an orgy implies unbridled sensuality with the females participating as fully as the males, real sensuality is not present in group rape. Sensuality takes leisure and concentration, a finesse in feelings that includes some recognition of the reactions of the person with whom the experience is shared. Group rape, even if it involves fellatio and cunnilingus or other forms of experimentation, is as rudimentary in its satisfactions as in its philosophy. Some participants admit later that it was not an enjoyable experience. Especially at the end, when the victim is exhausted and filthy, the last ones get no more than "a dead body." In general, only those with a really perverse erotic taste will continue to take part in group rapes. Most members conform once, out of allegiance to the group, and never rape again. Group sex, however, may remain a common experience until, when the men are in their late twenties, more conservative patterns take over.

The elements that attract and hold members to the group are also those that make possible the event of group rape.

Freud believed that the value for a group to its members was erotic in nature, that its ties represent the libidinal ones of the family. He held sexuality to be an inherent element of the group's thought and processes. Certainly it is a primary one in the dynamics of the gang that turns to rape.

Rape is generally a crime of youth; group rape, especially, is particular to men under twenty-five. The young American male in all social classes is troubled by two urgent problems. Maturing sexually, he is thrust into a new role, biologically, for which society makes no provisions. It not only denies outlets for needs that nature clearly intended to be fulfilled, it pretends to ignore that they exist, offering instead a puritanical ethic of waiting through a prolonged education or apprenticeship until a financial basis for marriage is laid. This is often youth's first introduction to the blind and arbitrary limits of the society in which he is going to have to find his place as a man. He is obliged to choose between being true to his own urgent nature and conforming to the standards of a social order that shows no concern for the facts of humanness. Inevitably he wonders, "Why am I having these urges if I'm not supposed to? Am I wrong . . . or they?" On all sides he gets the message that he is becoming a man and must prepare to act as one. Yet he is denied the right to discover himself as a male. His need to experiment in his new role becomes his most urgent problem, yet, legally, he cannot.

At the same time he is under pressure to decide on his work, the means of livelihood on which his future depends. But his confidence in himself and his ability to make decisions is buffeted by rules that put down what is of most importance to him at that moment: his sense of his own new manhood.

During this difficult stage, sports and studies are encouraged in upper-class families. In lower-class communities, where alternatives are few and precept and example are often lacking, the youth frequently looks for sexual identity through membership in a gang. With others of like background he unites around a leader who epitomizes the qualities they most admire. This leader serves as a means of resolving their conflicts about sexuality and aggression. Within the gang the youth shares the frustrations, shocks, and disappointments of his age. Finding that he is not alone is a balm; a conspiratorial unity against the unfair outer world seems deeply satisfying. The leaders replace his parents; his peers become his brothers in a fraternal loyalty. Better than any other institution or device the gang seems to provide what he craves.

Often the gang engages in activities that, in their sexual sadism, resemble the puberty rites of primitive tribes. Members prove their nerve and sexual potency to themselves and the others in fierce tests. Under the new code of the gang, personified by a leader who successfully expresses what the others feel, the youth's desires are validated and his conflicts healed.

A homosexual element is implicit in the relations within these gangs. This may seem a contradiction with the youth's need to explore his new-found masculinity but in fact is not. The strange new processes taking place in his body, altering his appearance and giving him new desires, makes him hyperaware of his own person, and by extension, of his peers, whom he studies with an interest that borders on the obsessive. During this phase (which usually, in a few years, passes without trauma into heterosexual interests) youths worry about and glorify their own and each other's physiques and exploits unendingly. Elements of a homosexual nature in their group life at this time include colorful or provocative attire, masturbation together, and constant concern for body and appearance.

Sexual desires are relentless, but experience with the opposite sex seems to the youth full of peril. He is seized with a loathing for what he perceives to be an insidious enemy. Within the family he rejects his mothers and sisters; he mocks all that is feminine. He delights in being abominable to everyone who doesn't possess a magic penis like himself and obnoxious to everyone else who does. During this painful period his greatest—sometimes his only—satisfaction comes from the interaction of his group.

In their sexual activity, as in all else, these members who rely on one another as a hedge against outside threat unite also. There is too much risk in facing a female alone; to reduce the danger they share a common sexual object. Participating in front of one another is very close to participating *with* one another. It contains elements of seeing and feeling "sex with a male." All the feelings that members are capable of at that time are oriented toward one another, and this is expressed, even if not directly, by sharing their sexuality. The sex object, whose significance as a person has been neutralized, symbolically represents each other. In group sex, or better still, in group rape, for then they are not in any way beholden to the female, they express for the first time their feelings of identity with another person through sexuality. And at the same time protect themselves against forming relations with the opposite sex.

When a criminal activity such as group rape is planned, a member may not wish to take part, some of his fears, such as that of being caught, being quite valid. Why then would he participate in an event that makes him feel fearful and guilty?

The explanation lies both in the psychology of the individual who joins the gang and in the process of the group itself. The gang is made up of individuals who, by seeking membership, show themselves predisposed to its influence. Each one brings to the group a supplement of the ideas that already prevail and that, by being shared with the group, are certified and reinforced. Even if these ideas run counter to those of the majority culture in such matters as sex and attitudes toward women, they take on a cachet of approval. The gang not only overcomes objection to these ideas; it provides new mechanisms for justifying them.

Gang members are not controlled by commands from their leaders. The group operates under a strong set of "oughts," a code of what one should do and feel that emanates from the body of the group and is independent of individual wishes. These "oughts" include a sense of loyalty and willingness to sacrifice personal desires for the group's needs. When action for the group is decided on, it is the pressure of these "oughts," stronger than any command (which at this stage of contrariness a member might well resist) that obliges him to conform.

If the member has doubts about an antisocial act like rape, these "oughts" present another complication in the dilemma of his conflicting desires. First, there is the conflict between his sexual-aggressive wishes and the controls that society insists he exercise over them. Then there is the conflict between his personal wishes and those of the group. His desires must thus work through three successive stages: "I'd *like* to perform this ultra-male act, though I *shouldn't* because all the outside rules say it is *wrong*. But even if I'm afraid and *don't want* to do it, I *should*, to please the Group, which is *right*."

In group rape the planning is of great importance. Preliminary discussions allow feelings to be ventilated and excuses improvised. As the members talk and decide that the idea is a good one, the group's courage is raised. With his guilt neutralized in the sharing, the individual's personal restraints are dissolved; he is ready to act.

The psychological explanation of the fearful member's conforming against his will is even simpler. Whatever anxiety he may feel about the project, his fear of finding himself alone, outside the group, is worse. The gang also engages in a number of noncriminal activities, and these help to reduce the member's anxiety and guilt.

Although it may affect his status with the others, a member can opt not to comply. He is not a captive of the group, constantly subject to its requirements, even though he may often feel so. Faced with the event, he may refuse to participate or even to witness; or he may, although negative at the outset, be converted. A member may be so frightened by the struggles of the victim and the violence needed to subdue her that he cannot have an erection. He may sense the homosexual element and be disturbed by it, or he may be capable of sexual action but be unwilling to force relations on a victim for whom the odds are so clearly unfair. The female chosen may be the one whom he does not consider permissible as a victim. Occasionally a member will try to dissuade the others: "Don't do it, you're crazy."

These conflicts, which may be experienced to a greater or lesser degree by everyone in the group, can often be resolved by the actions of one of the other members with whom they identify. By carrying out the first, instrumental act and showing that the sky doesn't fall, he breaks down inhibitions, he seduces the others into following. This is a form of leadership, although it may not be supplied by the group's usual leader.

Besides this "initiator," another member who helps to precipitate the group's act is the "bad influence." The lack of inhibitions in his exuberant and apparently unconflicted personality helps to resolve the conflicts of others. He does not lead but infectiously supports the event by supplying an energy and sense of ease to it.

A third kind of central personality is that of the organizer. He proposes the idea, has suggestions as to how it can be carried out, and may even strike the first blow or go on the victim first. His acts, however, do not have the same effect on the others as those of the "seducer."

For the law, it is important to understand which participants played which roles, in order to determine responsibility in the event. If the gang is caught, the member who declined to participate is usually the easiest for the police to get to talk. If all the members stick together on their story that the girl consented, then it is difficult for the law to prosecute, unless the victim can prove brutality. However, if the police can get one member to admit that the girl was coerced, then the whole gang can be charged.

Legally, the nonparticipant who remains with the group during the rape can be charged with complicity in the act. The same purpose and intent are assumed to him. (Time ran out? Low man on the totem pole? Wanted to but couldn't function?) He may receive a sentence not much lighter than those who participated fully.

There are probably no groups that exist solely for the purpose of carrying out gang rapes, not even the Hell's Angels. Most unorganized gangs have no other function than to provide a camaraderie based on similar psychological age and neighborhood contiguity. Gang members live within walking distance of one another; easy frequent access to each other's company, which makes the relationship seem comfortable and without strings, is essential. Younger boys tend to meet at neutral neighborhood facilities like drug stores and playgrounds; in the large tenement buildings of inner cities they often meet in the stairwells. Older youths with more money and mobility graduate to skating rinks, car and cycle repair shops, kung fu gyms, wherever there is an interest of their age group to serve as a focal point, or, lacking that, an unconfining semipublic place where they can meet without being hassled by other age groups. In the army and navy young soldiers and sailors find compatible buddies with whom, as a group, they share every possible experience during their term of service together.

Across the nation, spontaneously and without design, wherever numbers of youths get together, these informal gangs develop. Generally their purposes are innocent; they provide safe relationships within which to work out male roles and attitudes. For a few months or a few years—sometimes only a summer or the season of an activity (surfing, drag racing)—the gang blooms, then dissolves as work, school, or the family situation of members changes, or their need for the gang diminishes.

Organized gangs of subcultures are quite different. Mere camaraderie does not suffice; they are prestige-oriented, bent on making their mark with peer groups. This takes the form of belligerently staking out territory, then defending it in what may turn out to be murderous gang wars. However, organized gangs represent only a small fraction of all the youths involved in gangs, and their rivalries are particular to certain cities—like Philadelphia—where conditions have been breeding these anomalies for a long time.

Still, every group of youths in these dangerous years has a potential for trouble. If a once tight-knit, rewarding gang seems to have lost its spirit, and its leadership is predisposed to antisocial acts, then a group rape may seem a good way to revive enthusiasm. The membership, prescient to its own needs and with remarkable unanimity, may make the preliminary moves for a "gang bang."

(Studies on rape often use the terms "gang bang" and "gang shag" interchangeably although technically in a "shag" the girl is willing. Pack rape is another term. Names are often drawn from sportslike images. In France it is a "rodeo"; in Australia a "backup," a rugby term. "Lineup" is from American football.)

Tension among members runs high during a group rape. After the decision has been reached the group usually engages in a number of nervous preparatory rituals such as drinking—although getting drunk is not the goal—and prowling about on foot or in cars, studying potential victims. They joke, brag, quarrel among themselves, provoke outsiders, do whatever is necessary to raise the current of energy into a binding, focused will that involves them all.

Group rapes tend to be weekend, nocturnal affairs; they take place on Saturday more than twice as often as on any week night except Friday, which is slightly behind Saturday. Sunday is a weak third. If the event is out of doors there is always the danger of being discovered. Sometimes it is carried out on a mattress in an alley or cul-de-sac, guarded by members who can deflect straying passersby. A truck or the back seat of a car in a lonely warehouse has often served; dark corners near subways where the noise of frequently passing trains can block out the victim's commotion have been used. (The people of such neighborhoods often pay no attention to *any* kind of noise.) If the countryside is not too far out of town the gang may drive there, to fields, woods, or beaches. Rarely patrolled cemeteries and city dumps are classic locations. In big cities, lofts and garages are commandeered.

When group rape takes place in a house or apartment there is more privacy during the sex act. Usually the men take turns entering the bedroom where the victim is; only a few use the event exhibitionistically, to show that they can get off with others watching, or to satisfy voyeuristic impulses. Occasionally, however, there is coaching; participants badger one another or watch a shy member, to see if he can function.

An event held in a secure locale may last for several hours, during which time members may come and go, make telephone calls, and secure drinking supplies, pot, or hash. New units, invited or uninvited, may arrive, to be accepted or driven off. There is a lot of nervous ragging, occasionally some scuffling, even a dustup. Quarrels break out over trifles; alliances within the group may be strengthened or shattered. Usually members do not take off their trousers; waiting their turn they unzip their flies and massage themselves, circulating restlessly. They prod one another to hurry, afraid they'll lose their hard or that the bang will be interrupted before their turn comes. The one who takes a lot of time will be goaded: "Finish, finish!"

Relationship with the victim is minimal. Less than a person, she is hardly even a sexual curiosity; the members are more concerned with their own sexual organs than hers. It is not she who is an erotic instrument, who stimulates them, as much as it is their own excitement in sharing this male exploit. Her personality, femininity, physique are of no real interest. Acknowledgment of her humanness rarely goes further than a remark or two, more amused than regretful, like "The chick really got it. Her cunt won't work for months." Mostly they regard her with the insensible interest a rifle marksman shows for the circles on the target.

At first the victim may be held by the shoulders and feet. After two or three have passed there is no further need to hold her. In order to attain extra prestige members may contrive bizarre indignities to add to the rape. As if penetration and oral sex were not enough, as if slapping, hitting, and kicking were not enough, they include such extravagant defilements as the use of excretory functions.

Group rape cannot be isolated from the total social pattern in which it occurs. If it were radically different from what the members were accustomed to, they probably could not function. Group rape does not appeal, for instance, to young men whose views about sex are romantic, private, and conservative. Neither does it appeal to men who are past a certain age, for experience brings with it reticences and reservations. It would be inconceivable, for example, for a group of bank presidents to participate in a group rape.

Groups that rape take their tone from a cultural matrix in which, as was pointed out earlier, sex is not associated with emotions or privacy and women are little more than a receptacle for the act. These ideas are not born with the youths' first impulses about sex but are established long before, in the child's family life. Most ✓ attitudes about sex and sex roles come from family talk and the feelings members show for one another. An adolescent's ideas about females derive more from the way he has seen his mother treated by his father or by other mature males than from what he learns at school or from any other source, with the possible exception—in homes where the parents are gone a lot and the TV is on a lot—of the invidious influence of television.

Attitudes about sex are closely related to attitudes about aggressiveness. Adolescence is often characterized by increased aggressiveness, and adolescents from the lower socioeconomic groups are particularly prone to aggressive acts. In their communities, ripe with frustration, violence is commonplace. The speech of the people is violent in image and peppered with threats. Sporadically these threats are carried out in all kinds of crimes against the person. Conditioned as they are, youths have only to attain the necessary size and strength and they feel free to act out their aggressiveness.

The ages ten to nineteen are the prime years for delinquency, especially gang delinquency, and these are the ages during which group rape most often occurs. In Dr. Menachem Amir's comprehensive Philadelphia study, which involved 1,292 offenders, more than half, 712, were group-rape offenders, and more than half of these, 397, were nineteen years old or less. The youngest offenders in this study, between ten and fourteen years of age, were involved in either pair or group rapes, none in single attacks. It is not necessary to be able to sustain an erection or to have an emission in order to be charged with rape. If a male penetrates, he is guilty. Often these youngsters convict themselves when they brag to the police about taking part in an event. About one third of the group offenders were between twenty and twenty-four years; one sixth were more than twenty-five years of age. Leadership was almost equally divided, proportionally, between the three age groups.

The peak years for group rape are ages eighteen and nineteen. Few offenders are married at this age, although many have more or less regular sexual activity. Youths in the lower economic groups often leave school early to work, and the first major purchase of these early earners is likely to be a car. This provides a new freedom and range of activity; dragging the streets for girls becomes a prime distraction. The car has been blamed for everything from the rise in illegitimacy to the decline of the horse, and it does, in fact, play a part in many group rapes, if not actually as the place where they are carried out, at least to transport the victim to a safe locale. In Amir's study, the greatest number of group rapes took place where one of the participants lived. The rest were situated in almost equal numbers either in an automobile, out of doors, or indoors but not where a participant lived.

Alcohol plays a role in group rape, as in single rape. In a victim its visible presence makes her an appealing target; in the offenders it neutralizes restraints, fogs judgment. Among group-rape leaders, 53 out of 171, almost one third, had used alcohol; among members, 118 of 541, or a little more than one fifty. Almost half the victims had house where neighbors are well removed or unlikely to intervene, is with the group, some having drunk before they encountered the group. Plying a potential victim with drinks to lower her resistance is more common in single rapes; a group can obtain compliance in more direct ways. The use of hash is also common in group rape, although there are no statistics on this.

Planning the event takes place more often in groups (seven-eighths of the cases in Amir's study) than in single attacks (a little more than one half). This is an important preliminary for the group, in which members assess one another's spirit, test the gang's unity. Sometimes the victim is decided in advance and then a place, such as a house where neighbors are well removed or unlikely to intervene, is sought out. At other times the locale is available and the victim is the object of several hours' search during which the rising tensions within the group become important in forging its purpose. Occasionally the event is half planned: a female who seems appropriate strays into their territory at a time when the group needs action. The chance is recognized and communicated among the members. Since gang activities are episodic, the group that rapes may comprise not the whole membership but a handful who unite for this event or who are mobilized by an opportunity that seems irresistible.

Amir's study revealed group rape as largely an intraracial crime. Black offenders who raped black victims numbered 590, while only 11 blacks raped white victims; the proportion is one in almost sixty. There were 99 white offenders who raped white victims and 12 who raped black victims, or about one in eight. Whites crossed racial lines about seven times as often as blacks. Black offenders took part in group events five times as often as whites (601 to 111) in five times as many cases (143 to 28). There were an average of four offenders at each event for both races.

The arrest records of group rape offenders were not as bad as those of single offenders. Only one out of eight group-rape offenders had a criminal record while one out of four offenders in single rape had been arrested earlier. This supports the distinction in the psychological differences between single and group offenders: while the offender who rapes alone tends to be neurotically compulsive, often a repeater, the group offender is usually acting in response to his cultural pattern. The leaders in group rape tend to be a more hardened, asocial type than their followers. They have more previous offenses (one out of four) than their followers (one out of twelve). Because leaders are more of a threat to society than their followers, it is important for investigating officers to determine who the leader in each gang is.

Although the leader is, theoretically, the person with the greatest influence over the group, he may or may not be the one who leads in a rape. In Amir's study, only 6 of the 171 rapes were committed by stable, organized gangs. In each of these it was the leader who struck first, but in only three of these cases did he rape first, a clever move for a leader who wants to decline leadership in case of arrest. It can also be a political move for him to let an edgy member capture the momentary prestige of this initiative. If not first, the leader of the group is never far behind. To keep his primacy he must take the victim before she becomes too broken in spirit, too disgustingly oozy with semen—in effect, spoiled goods.

The most important fact to be found in the previous criminal records of group rape offenders is that seven out of eight have not been arrested, are unlikely to have raped before, and probably will not rape again. With the exception of some leaders, the youth who rapes in a group is not much different from other youths of that age who do not rape.

Group rape is not, as has been suggested, a group of youths banding together to achieve what one could not do alone. Neither is it a collection of individual rapists who get together to rape, as a group of bird watchers get together to watch birds. Not all the groups that rape are the same.

Most juvenile gangs are noncriminal in their orientation. Although their leaders may be more unprincipled, most youths will evolve through the stage of group life into conventional members of society. The group provides possibilities for sharing many experiences, and sexual adventures are a part of this important sharing. The mood is more experimental than sadistic. However, once the group moves to act, its image is at stake; any threat to its prestige can be ruthlessly put down.

The most dangerous groups are the organized gangs of youths who have already collided with the law. Their leaders are cynical and heartless, with grim records of crimes against the person to prove it.

These gang members can be described as "crime junkies," personalities that occasionally need the "fix" of a crime with its attendant risks and asocial satisfactions. Crime, like dope, is habit-forming. Once begun it is not easy to find other satisfactions to replace it. These young men with serious police records are survivors, and because of this their acts are both more calculated and more defiant. They know what criminal "justice" has to offer and hardly care. Outlaws each, they are united by pasts that already shadow their futures; they use the present with a cynical disdain—what have they to lose?

Finally, there are unorganized groups that rape—three or more young men who are thrown together for a weekend or an evening: servicemen on leave, the leftovers from a drinking party, or a group that has become congenial in a bar and decides to look for action, preferably sexual. (So many encounters between offenders and rape victims take place in front of a bar that Amir made a separate category for it, as distinct from other encounters on the street.)

In these ad hoc groups that have little or no continuity of relationships, the pack spirit is not the motivating force for conforming; rather it is an individual need to show well before the others. This may come closer to being a series of individual rapes; still the influence of the other is important enough to make the total event a cohesive one, with the reinforcement of the group amounting to more than a series of individual performances. In "party rapes" there is often no real violence. Toward the end of an evening, a group that has gathered for other purposes narrows down to a few like-minded men who focus on an available woman. Although not actually brutal, they harass her, will not let her leave. Finally, worn down by fatigue and perhaps alcohol, fearful of the potential menace in the number of her tormentors, the woman succumbs.

Weapons are rarely needed, or used, to subdue a victim. The mere number of the group is usually enough to overcome her resistance, although sometimes she does fight, depending on her age, race, and temperament, and whether or not she has been drinking, as well as the mood and appearance of the attacking group.

In Amir's study about one half the victims immediately submitted to the group, about one third showed some resistance, and fewer than one sixth actually fought. In single rape, even more—about three fifths—were submissive, with one fifth resisting and one fifth fighting. The assumption is that with the group the victim felt in greater danger; desperation lent courage. More than with a single offender she may have felt that her very life was in jeopardy. In single rape, about 50 percent of the victims know the offender, many very well. While they may feel that they cannot stop the rape, they do not feel that the offender would go so far as murder.

The amount of brutality in a group rape depends to some extent on whether the gang knows the victim or not. The pickup with a bad reputation is the most brutally treated. If she is known to participate in group sex, if she is of ill repute in the neighborhood, then she is an acceptable victim and the group's contempt can take cruel forms. They know they are safe from prosecution; no court that learned of her reputation would agree to hear her case. This victim is usually of the same subcultural group as her offenders; rarely is she of a different class or neighborhood. Like them she is young; more than half the offenders are within five years of her age. (In single rape the victim is often ten or more years younger or older.) Although she is usually under twenty-one, she is not a child. Whereas the single offender, in his neurotic search for someone vulnerable (and often for someone of his own mental age), will seize a child of thirteen, ten, or even younger, the group, which is not neurotic, seizes a more worthy and acceptable victim, usually a sexually experienced victim of its own kind.

A different kind of victim is the one who is "accidental," an innocent passerby with nothing provocative in her behavior who may be seized because she is in the gang territory. An unknown drunk or drinking woman is also a likely target. It is highly unlikely that a gang would seize a mature "straight" woman, a blue-haired dowager or suburban housewife with her shopping lists. Such victims would be sure to report, and the gang is not looking for *criminal* activity so much as tension-releasing, prestige-building adventure. The group's instinct is not self-destructive; on the contrary, most of its activities are useful both for the individual and the gang.

Another kind of victim is the one who changes her mind after agreeing to sex with several youths. Sometimes she is the sexual partner of a gang member, who, to consolidate his position within the group, agrees to share her with them. The girl may find herself roughed-up, treated with a contempt she had not expected, or faced with an additional carload of players. From compliant accomplice the girl may be transformed into a terrified and furious victim.

Police are reluctant to get involved in such a case; district attorneys know that the chances for getting a conviction are nil. "What jury is going to take seriously a charge that the first guy was for love, the next two for kicks, and all the rest were rape?"

Because this victim is usually from the same background as her offenders, the experience, however painful and frightening to her, is not as shocking as it would be to a sheltered, middle-class victim who has not matured in a climate of impersonal sex and the female put-down. The victim may be outraged to find friends of her brother's in the lineup on her, but she probably knew a lot about such events before it happened to her.

A variation of this type is the accidental victim who finds the gang closing in on her; she agrees to submit to one or two of them in the hope that she will be spared by the others. She soon finds how mistaken she was.

There is little hope of escape for a victim seized by a gang. It is useless, says Amir, for a victim to look for a member who appears more sympathetic than the others to save her. The one with the least taste for violence or exploitation will also be the least equipped to take a position divergent from the group. The esteem of the gang and his position in it are more important to each member than the fate of the victim or he would not be involved at all.

The pattern for group rape is often set by girls who attach themselves to juvenile gangs as fringe members. Like the boys, they seek from the gang what they could not get at home in affection or recognition. Like them they are in need of adventure, unsure of their own identities, and confused about an appropriate sexual role. Their needs are more emotional than sexual. They need an entity they can belong to and show loyalty for.

These girls are more disturbed than their male counterparts. They need a higher degree of alienation in order to do the things that are normal for boys of that age. The way to achieve acceptance by the gang, they find, is to become available for group sex. The go-to-hell brass with which they accept this function only confirms the gang's opinion of sex as a good joke on females. "Sexual consent" has nothing to do with the meaning given to it in middle-class circles. Here, the girl's mere presence is a form of consent, an acceptance of the gang's attitude toward sex.

In these mixed gangs there is a lot of jostling and scuffling, continual horseplay of an aggressive nature. Members hit one another; if girls are there, they hit them with equal abandon. In this context of easy, rough body contact, sex is a common, casual event regarded as a natural right. Rape, in its inflammatory definition for the middle class, is unknown.

One other group-rape victim whose case does not reach the courts is the girl who has hung out with a gang like the Hell's Angels, in which she must take on the whole membership as an act of initiation. If, later, she dishonors the Angels or a member in some way, she may be chastized by again being forced to "pull the Angel train." Gang rape, even the Angels admit, is ugly; they use it as a punishment. With them it acquires ritualistic overtones, like the purging of a witch. It is not done in the back of a pickup truck, where much of the Angels' group sex takes place, but in a clear area where everyone can watch, including the "old ladies" (regular partners of members) and "mamas" (female followers who will take on any member at any time), although most of these women prefer not to witness such shows. The punishment is carried out by the wronged Angel and others who have a taste for this sort of thing. These are, according to Hunter Thompson, who wrote of the Angel gangs, the meanest of the lot, the ones who are unpredictably hostile in all kinds of situations.

Although most group rape is straight intercourse it can also include such acts as fellatio, cunnilingus, and sodomy, all of which Amir lists as "humiliation to the victim," together with repeated acts of intercourse. There was no sodomy in the groups of the Philadelphia study. Since sodomy occasionally takes place in rape by a single offender (because the woman is menstruating, or by the choice of the man), this raises a question about the unwillingness of men to be witnessed in what is essentially a homosexual act. Or is it that the homosexuality implied in the shared sexual object is all that the group can accept? At any rate, it suggests that there are sexual acts that men will perform when alone with a victim that they do not feel are acceptable in a group. In 370 single cases there were 9 acts of sodomy, about 3 percent.

Fellatio was required of the victim in 88 acts, slightly more often (one out of seven) than in single rapes (one out of twelve.) There was no case of cunnilingus alone, although it was not uncommon together with fellatio among group-rape followers (one out of six); only one of the 171 leaders engaged in it, however.

Oral sex has strong symbolic overtones. These statistics seem to suggest that it is acceptable in a group to perform oral sex on a woman if she also performs oral sex on the man, but not unless she does. In spite of the slavish subjection implied in fellatio it was not required of the victim (one out of seven) more often than the man was willing to perform oral sex on her.

However, the meaning of oral sex performed on a woman in group rape is very different from its meaning between consenting individuals. In a group it may be related to curiosity and a desire to experiment sexually; often it is a performance for the benefit of the others. It may be a testing of nerve, a proof to one's self and one's peers, or it may be simply to follow a pattern established by an earlier member. One of the stories the Hell's Angels circulate about themselves is that a test of membership is to perform cunnilingus on a heavily menstruating female, in front of the gang, as a proof of "class."

Intercourse was performed more than once by one out of four leaders but only by one out of six followers. This may reflect the leader's ascendancy in preempting what he wished while some of the others did not have time for a second turn. Or it may express the leader's feeling that he must outdo the membership. In single rape, more than one intercourse was performed by one out of twelve offenders. In pair-rapes, about one out of ten.

Amir also lists use of a prophylactic under "humiliation to the victim," finding in this fastidiousness a bitter irony: the offender doesn't want any bad aftereffects for himself, like a social disease, from the women he forces. Six of the six hundred and one group offenders used prophylactics, about the same proportion as for single rapes (3 of the 370).

Leaders did not always humiliate the victim the most. In fact, 114 leaders out of 171 did none of these things. Among followers, fewer than half engaged in these humiliations.

Although witless and cruel, the behavior in group rape is not psychotic. When seen as an extension of the prevailing or "normal" attitudes of subculture members, it is no longer bizarre. For them it is just "good, dirty fun," as Groucho Marx put it. Whereas a plea of insanity is often used for the single offender, it is never used as an excuse in group rape.

Group rape has a potential for terrible brutality. Most group violence, however, is likely to be symbolic rather than serious. Broken bones and repeated stabbings, evidence of psychopathic disturbances, are not present here. There is a lot of roughness and nonbrutal beating: slapping, pushing around, and pinching. Members pinch the victim not only to share in touching her flesh, but to torment her into response; it serves the same purpose as the pricking of the sacrificial bull to greater action by the *picadores* of the *corrida*. While a soft pinch can be a teasing love token, a mean pinch has a certain cannibalistic element to it; it simulates ripping off flesh as for a morsel to nibble. In this the group event even takes on ritualistic overtones, the sharing of food being one of the earliest rituals observed by man.

Brutal beating can take place both before and after rape, but it is the exception rather than the rule. There is also choking by both the leader and the followers, especially the former. However, four out of five followers in Amir's study used no violence at all on the victim. This can be explained in several ways. It was not necessary because she was already subdued by the leader (nineteen out of twenty of them used force) or because the victim, intimidated by their numbers, submitted immediately. There were also cases where the violence was not to the victim but to her male companion. When he was attacked and beaten unconscious, nothing further was needed to arrange her compliance.

As has been emphasized earlier, what takes place in group rape is a reflection of the culture in which it takes place. In Germany, where a free-swinging violence is commonly associated with drinking, group rape has included acts of sadistic brutality, the members urinating on the victim and inserting foreign objects such as bottles into her. In France there were several cases in which the group tried to tape-record the event. One French group found its victim too submissive and insisted that she pretend a show of resistance.

Group rape does not end in murder. When a rape victim is killed it is because the offender has panicked and tried to destroy the evidence of his deed. In group rape the guilt is neutralized in the sharing; there is no need to harm the victim further. Sometimes she is given a roughing-up before being released, to convince her that she shouldn't report. At other times this is not considered necessary; she has even been returned to her home in a show of consideration based on confidence that she would not turn the group in.

It takes great courage for the usually young victim of a group rape to report the event to police. Not only because of the grotesque obstacle course she will be put through by the law but because she knows that for each offender she points out, usually from her own neighborhood, there may be a buddy to avenge him. For all its prevalence in police statistics, group rape may be one of the most underreported crimes.

Group rape is more explainable than individual rape. There is more logic to it, it makes more sense. When a man rapes alone, he neither gets love nor really expresses hate. He tries to seize something that cannot be seized and in the act deprives himself of its true essence. What should be a satisfying sensual experience is twisted into a show of contempt; yet in expressing this the offender endangers himself both physically and psychologically. He puts his manhood on the line in a struggle that is neither necessary nor proof of anything. Even if he succeeds he gains nothing more than the pitiful spoil of bending an already weaker being to his will. When this counts for more than all the rest, then the victor is indeed a pathetic specimen of manhood.

Group rape, on the other hand, for all its atrociousness, does serve a purpose. It is depersonalized, free of the strangling love-hate compulsions that drive the single offender. While it expresses scorn for females, especially certain kinds of females who appear to be appropriate victims, it is not the focal point of an individual fury, heated to the point of assault, as in a single rape. In group rape the offender acts out a prescribed role; by obeying the will of the group, he supplies a needed element of loyalty and solidarity for a social purpose, as he sees it. He is a socialized being, conforming to the needs of his social microcosm. The solitary rape offender, however daring he seems, knows that what he does is hateful not only to his victim but to society. He is an outlaw, not a member, a neurotic and lonely man, trying to find in the body of a woman who loathes him sustenance for a frantic and disfigured masculine ego.

As single rape is a psychological aberration, the cure of which lies in psychological treatment, group rape, a sociological aberration, requires a sociological solution. Dealing with the problem in a piecemeal fashion or focusing only on the negative aspects of this crime of youth will not serve. Account must be made of the youth amalgam as a whole, this distinctive entity with its special stresses and desires, potential and problems. Crime is a signal that help is needed. Crime is also a sign of neglected opportunity.

Each group rape is like the tip of an iceberg, revealing only a glimpse of the enormous store of youth's thwarted needs, anxieties, and rages, mostly unseen below the waters of social disapproval. For every crime that is reported there are several that are unreported and a thousand more in the daydreams of young men whose names will never be written on police blotters. Where there are criminal feelings there is a potential for crime. Inevitably there are breaks in the social membrane of restraint, and the handiest, most appealing target of all is often a female.

What can be done to meet youth's special requirements? When they reach an age when they crave adventure, can't bear the home nest, must test their nerve and will, are feisty with new sexual appetites, detest the opposite sex yet are secretly desperate to try out their fantastic new equipment, scorn their elders' authority while lacking the discipline to keep an order of their own—then, what is to be done with them? It can be an extremely dangerous age. "Adolescence," pronounced one psychiatrist who specializes in the subject, "is a state of insanity."

Passing through rituals of daring and pain is required of young men in primitive societies in order to achieve full manhood. These rituals show a sensitivity to the real needs of their members far in advance of that of the so-called civilized world, which is more likely to equip a youth with a 120-horsepower car and advise him to "be happy."

The success of nations in routing out millions of young men for service in the guise of national emergencies has proved that the military, with its masculine challenges and appeal to group loyalties and supra-ideals, meets many needs of these young men. Wars could not have achieved the popularity they have had (until recently) if they had not supplied many elements of satisfaction to those most involved in them.

But facile solutions are not the answer. Something better can be envisioned than youths proving their manhood by violating women and sacking weaker countries.

Youth's own answer to the torments of its age seems to be the group. What kinds of groups they evolve depend on the values of the surrounding culture. The society that seeks to rid itself of the horror of group rape must first change the attitudes within its culture that group rape reflects.

Youth groups can be as harmless and socially appropriate as any adult group that relies on some exclusivity for its appeal. They carry, in fact, far greater potential, due to the special capacity for enthusiasm and loyalty that youth's burgeoning social instincts bring to them. The positive elements inherent in the esprit de corps of the youth group could provide an admirable soil for learning to serve the larger causes of society.

The energy of youth, its ardor, idealism, and readiness to sacrifice, remain one of the still untapped great natural resources of the nation.

Suggested punishments for group rape have ranged from stiff prison terms to castration. Since the crime is not a neurotic act, the psychotherapy needed by the single offender is not the solution for these young men. Their attitudes toward females, however, and their asocial impulses should be reoriented.

Thoughtful criminologists suggest that group rape sentences

should not be overly harsh, only long enough to ensure that members will not reunite when released. Rehabilitation rather than vengeful punishment should be the aim of correction, especially for young offenders. Since most existing prisons are schools for crime, alternatives are needed for youths just above the juvenile limits. Group-rape offenders should be separated from one another, sent off to different areas of the country to work and learn in well-secured vocational training centers and in environmental projects similar to those of the old Civilian Conservation Corps camps. A complete change of ambience together with means of learning new skills would be far more constructive than traditional prison terms. Since offenders are usually eighteen or nineteen when they commit the crime, at the end of a two- or three-year term they have matured into other interests; the fascination of the old group no longer holds. For the great majority of young offenders this asocial behavior is episodic and particular to the stresses of their age; as they grow older it ceases.

In the meantime, what can be done to spare women the trauma of these rites of passage?

For all its journalistic shock effects, group rape remains the least studied and least understood of serious criminal offenses.

IV

PERSPECTIVES ON THE CRIME

15

Why Do Men Do It?

The crime of rape is only a small if spectacular manifestation of a much larger illness infecting the body of our population. Like eruptions in syphilis, the crime reveals a general infection that must be cured before the sores stop appearing. Treating the symptoms—rape offenders and victims—is only palliative. Is rape contagious? Why is it soaring to epidemiclike proportions? Is it really worse now, or is it just being reported more frequently? What can a concerned society do to control a crime that touches the lives of more and more of its citizens each day?

An understanding of the causes of rape, of the general illness that it signals, is basic to any effort at reform. From time to time society has made abashed efforts at controlling what it perceived to be the cause of rape, without great results. In many of the ports of the world, like Marseilles and Hamburg, the town elders, believing that rape was based on sexual need, legalized prostitution in order to protect their wives and daughters from the floating populations of visiting seamen. But prostitution, it is now known, does not solve the problem. Rape is not simply a means of obtaining sexual release, and the man who wants to rape is not satisfied with a brothel.

Because the rate of rape in the United States, according to statistics, began to rise dramatically at the same time that controls on pornographic books and movies were relaxed, there have been attempts to prove that this has aggravated the crime, that "dirty books and pictures" make sex monsters. The diversity of standards in different parts of the United States makes it difficult to generalize about effects here, but in more homogeneous societies, as in Scandinavia, definite results can be noted. Denmark, for example, has reported a steady decrease in the number of sex crimes, particularly in child molestation and indecent exposure, since the lifting of restrictions on pornography. Although only 40 percent of the country was in favor of lifting restrictions at first, a year later nearly 60 percent were ready to agree it was a useful measure. Other Scandinavian countries have reported similar results. However, violence and exploitation are less common elements in these cultures. Because of old, well-established patterns, men are less likely to harm women or others weaker than themselves, and removing sexual barriers has not changed this tendency.

In the United States, which is the world capital of fantasy violence, however, disturbing reactions have followed movies that featured not just hard-core sex, but sex linked with violence. Movies that are sexually stimulating may increase sexual activity, but they do not encourage viewers into antisocial acts. There does, however, seem to be a contagious element in viewing violence and antisocial acts. Films in which men bang passive women around with a larky kind of contempt seem to imply that this kind of behavior is not only acceptable but normal. A viewer's antisocial impulses can be not only confirmed but stimulated; he may be encouraged to act them out.

It must be pointed out that movies do not *alter* people's personalities. A law-abiding, nonneurotic person will not become a criminal from seeing the enactment of a crime on the screen. If the desire to rob or rape is already there, however, a film can facilitate the expression of this desire. Movies, it has been noted, can teach criminal techniques to those interested in learning them. After the appearance of the film *Rififi*, in which burglars tunneled through a roof to steal jewels, police were confronted with a proliferation in this kind of crime. After the televised showing of "A Case of Rape," police agencies reported an increase in rape activity within twenty-four hours.

Judgments on films and books must make a careful distinction between material that stimulates sexual activity, which per se is not illegal, and material that stimulates antisocial acts, which are.

Feminist groups are apt to see rape as a symptom of a disease that is not so much a compound of ignorance and indifference as a male conspiracy to keep the levers of society in men's hands. Rape is viewed as an instrument of fear for keeping women off the streets and at home at night, and perpetuating their dependence on men for protection. Fear of rape thus becomes a means of protecting men's "property" as surely as a lock on a gate.

Rape has another symbolic function in an exploitative society. Since the offender's act is merely an extreme of a pattern that has the consent and approval of society, it is as if in punishing an offender society extirpates its guilt for its own immoral behavior, providing itself at the same time with a stolen-watermelon thrill. Its members have the vicarious pleasure of being stimulated by the details in the press, plus the satisfaction of denouncing and sometimes punishing the scapegoat that provided that pleasure. Fantasies are vicariously lived, purged, then repudiated. Society thus symbolically expurgates its obsession with the kind of exploitative behavior that the offender exemplifies, and individual guilty longings are exorcised by a common public scapegoat.

Because rape is a symbolic crime it is punished symbolically, and this is why it is so difficult to get a sane, detached appraisal in the court system. When rape no longer symbolizes the violation of female purity (thereby limiting the prosecution of the crime to cases in which society regards the victim as "pure"), then the crime will be prosecuted for what it is—an ugly attack on personal rights. But rape in itself is not a fate worse than death, it is not an affront to society's manhood any more than it is an offense against womanhood. It is a specific crime against a specific woman by a man who must be deterred from repeating the act, and if possible, rehabilitated so that the original motivations are removed. The crime of rape should be demystified.

While it is individuals who commit rape, society to a great extent determines the framework within which an individual chooses his acts. Therefore it is society's responsibility to redress the inequalities and hurts that produce the mental set leading to rape.

Rampant rape figures are the results of rampant frustration. The black man is the most frequent offender in U.S. crime records and he is also the most frustrated man in American society. Any real effort to reduce rape in the United States is going to have to take into consideration the problems of black people. Many rape studies dare not mention that 80 percent of the rape in the U.S. is by blacks, preferring, instead, to focus on the fact that 92 percent of rape is intraracial. As if rape were somehow more acceptable if confined to one's own people.

Politically enlightened blacks are trying to deal with the problem in their own communities. Besides working to improve frustrating conditions, they are teaching that rape is no way to settle for the white man's crimes against black women and the whole black race. Revenge is primitive and passé. If a black rapes a white, it is black women who are demeaned. The more militant disdain interracial relations as dishonoring their own color. Despite white racists' attempts to use the threat of rape by blacks to arouse terror, Amir's statistics show that offenses of black against white (3.3 percent) were slightly lower than those of white against black (3.6 percent). Considering the black woman's well-merited reluctance to try to prosecute a white man, this second figure is probably more token than real, probably representing ten times as many rapes by white men.

When the black community has an increased opportunity to improve conditions, its members will be less impelled to state their grievances through violence. The fact that their present displays of violence are mostly against their own people does not make the problem any less urgent. The cycle of rage and pain has to be broken. They will need to hurt each other—and others—less when they stop feeling hurt.

The war in Vietnam has had its fallout in the crime pattern at home. Many rape offenders are veterans of the conflict overseas, trained to violence, with the callousness of soul that techniques in violence require, and a ready contempt for the vulnerable and weak. It has also been suggested that many antisocial acts by veterans are a reflection of the rage they feel at being used in a hated war, sent out to kill or die by an unfeeling society that, although it condemned the war, did not stop it until several years and many thousands of dead later. Solving political problems with military action is an impressive lesson in the uses of violence to the young men who are required to fight.

The means for controlling the crime of rape in America should, logically, be inherent in an understanding of its causes. One thing is sure. It is no longer sufficient for treatises on rape to terminate with a few patronizing tips to women on how to avoid being attacked. Any serious attempts to deal with the problem are going to have to go far beyond this negative approach, which is basically an extension of the present sex-role Bait and Trap pattern. Popular articles that warn women not to walk alone in a park or on a city street at night are taking a coward's refuge in the simple solution. Not that any thinking woman, in the present climate, would take such risks, but what kind of a mentality assumes that vulnerability should automatically produce attack? As if controlling a desire to prey on the helpless were as impossible as reversing gravity! What kind of a society accepts man's most brutish instincts as irreversible and blames the woman for falling victim to them? Is this the kind of world we want to live in? Do we really want a society in which paranoia is not an illness but a necessary way of life?

What can be done to fight this disease within our culture? Increasing police protection clearly will not be useful since about half the participants know one another and more than half (56 percent) of the rapes take place in the home of either the offender or the victim. Obviously, the solution is going to have to be more far-reaching and complex than anything attempted so far. What can men, who hold the key roles in the functions of society and from whose ranks come the offenders, do about the crime? While the chief responsibility for change would seem to belong to them, it is a fact that women as well as men are accountable for the ethos in which violence and exploitation are accepted norms of behavior. Where have women failed? What must they do to overturn the old ways, install new ones? Could a psychopathology of relations between men and women hold the key to this crime in which sexual expression is the mode?

16

What Can Women Do?

Psychologically, the crime of rape is a baffling one. Inherent in the act are troubling and contradictory symbols derived from the deepest and most dangerous pockets of the human psyche. All crimes are loaded with components of primitive needs, but by comparison robbery, with its understandable element of gain, and homicide, as the overspill of heated emotions, seem almost simple.

Not only are offenders unable to control their impulse to rape, they do not seem to understand, themselves, why they do it. Men have been known to call a rape-crisis center and beg, "Help me! Give me a pill or something. I'm desperate."

One convicted offender in a state penal hospital told an interviewer, "I wish I knew why I did it. I was a successful businessman, but I raped at least a dozen times. In the middle of the night, lying next to my wife, I'd get so nervous I couldn't stand it. I'd get up and go prowling, find someone to rape. Sometimes I'd enter a house and go to the bed of a sleeping woman and not touch her. I'd stand there looking at her with tears running down my face. How do you stop yourself from doing things like that?" ·

Insight into the motives of rape offenders have rarely been provided by males who write splendidly about everything else. Authentic literary examples are rare. Jean Genet wrote of his homosexual rapes with an existential callousness: the inevitable plunder of the weak by the strong in the jungle of the half-world. Eldridge Cleaver wrote that his rapes, particularly of white women, were politically inspired, insurrectionary acts.

A look at the general psychology of the man who rapes might reveal clues to its causes. Let us reduce what is known of the most common type of offender to the simplest elements possible.

Given that you have a man with the classic background for the crime: that he's uneducated and works in an unskilled, badly paid job, if he has the luck to be employed at all, and that he's from a neighborhood where violence is standard fare and family relationships are often chaotic. Given that he's broke, unnoticed, unloved, lacking in self-esteem, and without any example for honesty, hard work, self-discipline, and the other middle-class virtues. Given that he's a sullen, unfulfilled, confused young man, furious with everyone he knows and especially with those who should be closest to him; that in his frustration and desperation he'd like to kill the world that has deprived him of half a chance to be the person he feels himself to be. Given all these elements, one can understand his desire to assault almost anyone, someone known to him or a stranger. One can imagine the satisfaction he would take in a deliberately antisocial act, burning up hostile energy in some forbidden deed. And one can see why he would choose to attack someone who was not only vulnerable but who symbolically seemed to be a source of a lot of his problems. Woman as an easy victim and a psychologically satisfying one has a certain logic. One can understand *the desire to assault*, and *the choice of target*. But why the *means*?

Why does this assault take the form of sticking his penis into her? Why, with all the angry movements that he could make—punching, kicking, butting, shaking, and slamming—why, with all the other parts of his body that he could use for aggression—fists, shoulders, feet, knees, and elbows—does he choose to expose his penis, this vulnerable, singular, almost magical possession, and engage it in an act of hate? In combat with another man, the groin area is one of the most instinctively protected. Why should this irreplaceable, masculine instrument be used to achieve his purpose? Why is the attack *sexual*? Why, if it is an act of violence and contempt, does it include that peculiar mystery in which two bodies are joined and the penetrating member achieves a release that is both exhilarating and pacifying at the same time?

It makes no sense. The elements are so contradictory, so peculiarly human, that they would be pathetic if such rage and pain on the part of the victim were not involved. Clearly, the man who rapes is trying to say something. Not directly to society, like a would-be suicide on a window ledge, for society may never know. Not even to the victim, for whom he often shows no regard, not even the interest of sadism. But to himself. The fact is, no matter what kind of an event it is—the accessory act of a burglar, a subcultural gang shag, or a stranger attack in the park—and no matter who the man is—poor, black, and angry, or white, middle-class, and neurotic—the offender is saying something about his manhood.

The man who rapes does so because he lacks a better means for making the point "I am a man."

The truth holds in every kind of case. It is true for the black man who has been emasculated by the white man's society and raised in a matriarchal family. It applies to the street gangs of young men in their rites of passage. It applies to the failed seduction, the bar pickup, the aging philanderer, the country bumpkin, the ex-con in a pair-rape, and the Berkeley youth who raped after he quarreled with his stepfather. It even explains the rape of the judge's daughter on the way to the movies. In his own weird way, the man who rapes is saying, "I need proof, I must test who I am."

While the need to test one's self is a staple of human behavior, it still is not clear why a man who is angry and confused in his relations with women would want to hurt them in *this way*. One additional element seems true in many though perhaps not all cases. This man secretly regards sex as degrading to women. In his anger with women, whom he considers base, unworthy creatures, he seeks to punish them by assaulting them in a degrading manner. This seems to apply especially to a compulsive type of middle-class white (brilliantly revealed in *Diary of a Rapist*) although less to blacks and teen-agers in their rites of passage.

Police have noted a change in the tone and patterns of rape in the last few years. It has become more violent, with new elements of humiliation. Demand for oral sex used to be rare in the crime; now it is almost standard. There used to be just enough violence to subdue a victim and to persuade her not to report. Now there are a lot of bizarre additional activities; it is as if forced sex alone were no longer vile enough. Once it seemed the ultimate abuse of human rights, the monstrous acting-out of a private fantasy. Now, with posters of twenty-eight sexual positions being sold in birthday-card shops and hours of hard-core films available in most major cities, mere intercourse seems to have lost some of its impact. These new elements of humiliation and brutality seem to confirm rape as a need to punish a woman by degrading her.

Doubts about one's manhood are not likely to go away without psychotherapy. The act of rape can become a habit, a regular "fix," needed like any other physical or psychological prop. Most offenders, if not stopped, continue to repeat the crime. Trapped in the myth of male supersexuality, the man who rapes must frequently retest himself to see if he fits the prevailing image of manhood.

(The feminine equivalent of this is the female who can't cease trying to prove that she is seductive. On the cocktail circuit she is a wearyingly familiar sight, with lots of cleavage, working her eyes on every man in range. Her impoverished ego needs its "fix" too. She must make men show that they find her sexually desirable. However, it is the chase, not the quarry, that interests her; she may or may not be an "easy lay." With the willfulness of a love goddess who is equal part spoiled brat she may refuse what her provocations promise. Her enraged partner, whether he resorts to violence or not, henceforth has a sneaky sympathy for the man who does, and the incident tends to supply ammunition for the male theory that the rape victim is an overseductive, undercompliant hussy. No matter how many times the woman is successful in attracting a male, it never really proves anything; at the next possible opportunity she will again need her "fix." Still, aggravating as her silly game is, it cannot be compared with the rape offender's brutality. Her behavior may add to the estrangement of the sexes but the pain is nothing like that of the battered, slashed rape victim.)

Crime is a sign of failure. It shows that the individual has failed to manage his life in a style acceptable to others, and it shows that society, which has a large part in the molding of each individual, has failed also in its task.

What can be done to reverse this tide of failures? The moral climate of the culture in which these failures take place might be examined first. The pressures that create rape continue to rise and the excuses for the man who chooses to rape are compounded daily in the examples of corruption and self-seeking ruthlessness that he can see at every level of life. There seems to be little hope for reducing the crime

—as long as exploitation of the weak by the strong and a disdain for any but material values remain the prevailing standards for "success";

—as long as male chauvinism is implicit in the laws, and the mass visual media regularly give a cachet of approval to establishing one's manhood by using a woman as a sex object;

—as long as the courts treat the victims with suspicion and disdain, as if *they* were the criminals, so that women are reluctant to endure the humiliation of a trial, and the real scope of the crime is not known;

—as long as the legal systems offer so little hope of conviction that the man who rapes knows he has a 99 percent chance of not being punished.

Attempts to prevent the crime might deal separately with the two aspects of the problem: the violence, and the sex.

Pleasure in all kinds of violence is a part of our ethos. Americans live in a culture of general violence that has several even more violent subcultures in which women are regarded as prey. This is not an inevitable part of metropolis-oriented living. There *are* nonviolent cultures, and not just primitive ones, either—the Swiss, for example. Most of America's violent subcultures are among the poor, with their related problems of illiteracy, malnutrition, illegitimacy, and unemployment. The classical remedies of assimilating the people in these subcultures, economically and socially, in opportunities for education, jobs, and decent housing must be implemented to eliminate the frustrations that produce violence.

Rape is not an abnormality in our culture; it is only an extreme of the accepted mode of male behavior. The man who rapes is not condemned for his attitude but rather for his failure to succeed in an otherwise accepted pattern. It is not that he has chosen wrong instead of right but that he miscalculated his odds for success in this particular instance. Crimes of exploitation are punished by society not to recompense the victim or even to punish the offender as much as to serve as a warning that society does not tolerate errors in judgment in certain matters. As long as aggressive, exploitative behavior remains the norm, it can be expected that individuals will make these errors and that the weaker members of society will be the victims.

"I really like men," said one angry speaker at a rape symposium. "They're my emotional center. But for two months after I was raped, if a man looked at me even a little bit funny I was ready to kick his balls in." This was not a militant Ms. speaking, this was a gay man. The shame, the fury are the same wherever one human is exploited sexually by another.

Lastly, rape is a crime of youth. Any real work on the prevention of rape has to take into account youth as a whole—the matrix of youth's ambitions, norms, and institutions. A piecemeal attack will be useless. Concrete and positive goals should include

1. Searching out, in junior high school or the upper levels of grade schools, those personalities that already show signs of being sick and alienated. Men who commit violent crimes have records as misfits while still very young. Psychotic individuals show symptoms as preadolescents or even as children. Trained school counselors could detect aberrant behavior, and treatment could begin early. Psychotherapy can work important changes at those ages. Many youngsters warped by a brutish home life can still be recuperated for a reasonably good adult life if given therapy in time.

2. Education. Education helps to reduce rape. It gives goals, teaches self-discipline, and imparts a sense of confidence. The individual with a constructive pattern for working out his doubts and frustrations is less likely to yield to the helpless, flailing, destructive pattern of the ignorant and untrained. Members of subcultures without means for adequate education cannot have the same goals and patterns as those who are well-educated.

3. Creative alternatives to military training, with its emphasis on violence, should be established for the formative years of eighteen to twenty. This training is often the first real socialization for a large group of young men, away from home for the first time, and could be a major chance to inculcate constructive instead of destructive attitudes and roles.

4. A more explicit sex education that does not attach shame to such practices as oral sex would be useful to young people. Most sex education is very vague and euphemistic, with only general references to "foreplay, kissing, touching . . ." Even worse for the rape victim than the intercourse is being told to put her hand or mouth on a man's penis. Sexually inexperienced victims are devastated when asked what happened. Even sexually mature women have wept bitterly, helplessly, in court, when told to describe what the offender made them do.

Some of the sexual humiliation inflicted on victims is the result of offenders trying to get what they can't get from their prudish wives or regular sex partners. If women were less inhibited with their men, the sense of depravity that their prudishness inspires might be reduced.

5. Most important of all for young men is an improvement of their attitude toward the opposite sex. As long as they are encouraged to believe that women are inferior, dependent creatures, asexual and stereotyped and therefore vulnerable to stereotype treatment, whether the man is rich or poor, educated or not, will matter little; he will conform to the accepted male role of the culture.

6. Women must be taught to take more responsibility in managing human relations. They have got to stop playing dangerous games, ignoring signals, and pretending they don't understand. Ignorance of the law is no excuse if you make a U turn on a city street, and ignorance of the laws of human nature is no excuse if you're going to function in society. Women can't ask men for a medieval chivalry while assuring them they are their equals. You can live in only one century at a time and there isn't much choice.

"I didn't think he would become aggressive just because I went to his apartment after a party," says one victim.

"It was raining and he was driving this nice Mercedes-Benz," says another.

"He was my girlfriend's old man—how was I to know he would turn violent?" How indeed!

This kind of hindsight lamenting no longer serves. Women who are serious about protecting themselves do not have such problems. They make a point of knowing what is on their companions' minds. "Hookers do not get raped," says Margo St. James, ex-prostitute and Chairmadam of the Coyotes, a loose women's organization in San Francisco. "They are on the streets late at night and in areas where there is a lot of crime, but they learn how to read signals, how to interpret body language. They can spot trouble well before it becomes trouble for them." Other women should learn to do the same.

Men cannot assume that they can have sex on demand how, when, and with whom they please, but they'll never be convinced of this as long as women keep putting themselves in compromising positions and asking for favors that establish a kind of "debt of vulnerability." Chief among these is hitchhiking. The hitchhiker asks for a service that has no equivalent compensation for the driver who gives it to her. One can talk all one wishes about the hitchhike ethic, but the fact is, there are still very few free lunches in the world as it is, and the woman who enters a stranger's car is making an open-end contract based on pure assumption on her part. Even if by good luck her assumptions of generosity and decorum are rewarded with astonishing frequency, the number of crime stories that have proliferated around the act show that her hopes are dangerously unrealistic.

The act of hitchhiking cheapens the value women seem to put on themselves. Either they want something for nothing, which is not the way the adult world works (only children get something for nothing), or they don't esteem their own persons enough to protect themselves. In either case they are selling womanhood short. They are perpetuating the myths of the dependent female and the female who permits her sexual experience to be decided by a man—and by any chance man, at that. It is not fair that a man, because he is physically stronger, should impose his will sexually. But several millenia of civilizing influences have not yet corrected this and probably won't for a while yet. In the meantime, women who are sincerely interested in lowering rape statistics will do all they can to teach their sisters not to hitchhike. What can be done to supply our mobile young nonmaterialistic population with a cheap and safe means of getting around is a problem that every community should consider.

It would be simple to think of women as the irresistible prey, the temptress, the Bait, and of the male's desperate sexual need for her as the Trap that ensnared them both. But such a metaphor would in fact illustrate the worst of the old dovetailing male chauvinist myths, exactly the error to be avoided.

The real Bait is far more subtle and insidious in its nature. The real Bait is the prize that is attached to woman's conforming to the desired female stereotype. It is her reward for fulfilling the male's desired image of her, at the sacrifice of her own nature. If she's passive, if she is nonsexual, fearful, and dependent on the male for protection, if she does not menace his sovereignty and in fact supports the myths that sustain this sovereignty, then she can achieve society's highest accolade for her sex: she can be known as "a good woman." As such she will merit the protection of the law and she will be eligible for a lifetime meal ticket who will also serve as the escort and defender that a "good" woman needs.

The myth that a woman's security lies with a man and that helplessness and passivity are among the necessary attributes to qualify contains a real Catch-22. In order to secure his protection she must make herself so weak that in fact she does need him to defend her.

This is the Bait with which women have been lured away from their independence and personal integrity. For the stability of a she-slave relationship, for a little sentimental swag and the booty of creature comforts in a protected existence, they have abdicated their rights; they have bought the package and sold it to their daughters, too.

The Trap is man's conviction that the present sex-role pattern is the best of all possible arrangements. Quite sincerely he believes that there are no suitable alternatives. Women were made physically weaker than men so that men could control them and women should have correspondingly weak characters in order to facilitate this control. He esteems these positions as God-given and irreversible; in acting as Lord and Chief High Pooh-Bah over lesser earthlings like women he is only fulfilling the divine order of nature. He can imagine nothing better than sex as a conquest (the word has entered literary form as such) and supposes it normal that his image of himself as a man should depend on his success in such conquests.

The anxiety, mismatching, pain, and loss for both men and women in playing out these inane prescribed roles are generally submerged in the hypocrisies of social machinery. Only in the more dramatic eruptions of crime are the twisted errors of the myths visible. Rape as an instrument for asserting the claims of these dear myths is obvious. Men who can't strike back at other men can always take out their rage on a woman in forced sex; that's all these dumb broads are good for anyhow.

Thanks to certain hobbling facts of nature, these ideas may have found no serious resistance in other epochs; it may even have been the better part of valor for those women who took their jobs as mothers seriously to play the men's game. To be generous, we may write off women's past mental indolence, prudery, and readiness to sacrifice moral responsibility as compromises "for the children's sake." But today, with the pill, education, economic mobility, and a new-found power at the ballot box, the old male truisms seem less and less like God's own design for the universe. The Trap is losing its snap. Are women now ready to resist the facile, foolish lure of the Bait?

17

What's in the Future?

"Why do women resist sex?" asked one puzzled offender, who knew his victim. "They like it. Why don't they relax and enjoy it?"

The man was wrong, of course, and the fact that he tried to force the woman was indefensible, yet his words fall close to a real truth concerning the psychology of the crime. He is saying he cannot understand why women are prudish and negative about sex when in fact he feels they should enjoy it and secretly do. He was questioning women's resistance to a frank sexuality, a resistance that in effect adds another element to sex, mystifies it, and often turns it into a power play that at worst can become rape.

As long as the idea of sex is one of "getting something from someone else," then it is the weaker from whom it will be taken. When it is an experience shared by two people and complete only when it is as rich for one as for the other, then it cannot be "seized" any more than a sunset or fine weather. Sex can and should be the ultimate expression of the willing gift.

As long as men regard sexual activity as "scoring" and hang their self-esteem on it instead of simply enjoying it, sex will remain a heavy burden for the male ego. The man who is unsure of himself will be desperate for an easy means to satisfy his need of proof. On the other hand, if women owned up to their sexuality and met men as equal partners, then the act would not only cease to be a conquest, it would lose the simpering, prudish tones that women have so often applied to it and that make sex seem degrading.

The hypocrisies in the double standards of our culture have reached levels that amount to sexual schizophrenia. In California, oral sex under any circumstance is a felony punishable by from five years to life in a state prison. Yet one can view this illegal activity for hours on end, in fifteen-foot-high close-ups at "adult" cinemas in most of its major cities.

And what is one to say about the Victorian prudery of a standard thesaurus, republished in 1963, that cannot bring itself to list the word "mate" as a verb? That does not contain the word "sexy" or even "sexual" as an adjective? And that lists intercourse only as "social," "friendly," or "verbal"?

Rape would lose much of its attraction if it were not thought of as

(1) a conquest, and (2) degrading to women. Women cannot win the battle against rape if they do not have equal sexual rights before the law. But women cannot have equal sexual rights until they have admitted to a sexuality that is equal to that of men. Until the pill, women were unable to express their sexuality as freely as men because they were shackled by the burdens of bearing and raising children. Now they have no more reason to deny their sexuality than do men; the sexual act need have no more penalties for them than for a man.

The unsexual woman has been an ideal of Western culture for so long that her opposite is hard to imagine. What would she be like, a woman whose sexuality was intact, who considered herself the sexual equal of a man on the job, socially, everywhere? How would she act, this woman who did not defer to males, who never simpered or wheedled but, like a self-confident man, stated what she wanted as if she expected to get it? What would she be like in bed? In their more reckless moments men have dared to fantasy such a creature, and the image was that of the fabled Amazon, muscular and voluptuous, larger than other women, larger even than her male companions. For a woman who was unafraid of her sexuality and could make sexual demands would loom very large; to many men she would seem threatening indeed.

The converse of the idea is equally striking. What is a man without his sexuality? A shrunken, withered drone, an inferior and pitiable human being.

One remembers a movie of the '30s in which a nervous matron, after studying Mae West's sultry walk and talk announced, "She doesn't look like a good woman to me." With good-humored contempt Mae swung a hip and countered, "Honey, I'm very, *very* good." The nuances of twenty centuries of double standards are in those two interpretations of the word "good." She enjoys sex: she's bad, she's dangerous. And the rejoinder: Why shouldn't I be pleased with my own sexuality?

For two thousand years the Christian world has made its obeisances to the most perfect of all women in history, a woman who gave birth to a son without losing her virginity. Ever since that miracle, and perhaps long before—since myths are an expression of a collective wish—this seems to have represented the ideal in womanliness: a female who can produce heirs while remaining totally ignorant of her own sexuality.

Why has female asexuality been sold as the apex of feminine virtue? Why is it that for women, less in sex is more—the less sexual she is, the more honored by both men and women? Why haven't women seen the myth of the supersexual male and the asexual female as a manipulative fraud, and rebelled?

In earlier centuries women had good reasons for accepting the myth, chief among them exhaustion from childbearing and the high mortality in childbirth. They did not want children as often as men wanted sex, and as soon as the two facts were connected, it became clear that the myth of asexuality had its advantages. The woman accepted therefore that the man seek his pleasure at times with a few "bad women" who were available for that purpose, while making it clear that the woman who provided what she refused was an outcast. Thus it was *women* who in their derisive scorn and jealousy contributed the most to the myth that the woman whose sexuality was in evidence was a "bad" woman. The idea of chastity also suited men, who did not want their women encumbered by other men's children while they were busy with the crusades or wars or whatever took them away for long periods of time; thus the virtue of asexuality, useful to both sexes, was established and reinforced. Religion, which has often served to prop up governmental authority, or any other authority useful to the functioning of society, added its support to the myth, and chastity acquired a mystique of honor, even divinity.

In order to have the security and stability they needed to bear and raise children women have accepted an unfair role, a false image, and the price has been a heavy one. Now *that is all past* and they have a chance to move into a new, creative, and self-fulfilling role in which they are equals with men on many levels. Only in brute strength is woman still man's inferior. But this, it is agreed by many people who have thought about the matter, is more than compensated for by her myterious personal powers: her ability to seduce, and her awesome ability to bring forth another human being. Women can now think of themselves as full partners in the human race, not merely the second sex.

Because of her influence on her children, it is acknowledged by many cultural groups that it is through the woman that their heritage is perpetuated. Is it not logical then, that it should be women who implement the needed changes for an enlightened culture? What can women, that enormously varying throng that make up more than 50 percent of the population and have the most to profit by change, do to weed out the old sick myths and to recast the stunted, stereotyped roles in which they have been trapped for so long? Couldn't this bring about the most important changes ever made in the relationship between the sexes?

Women's influence is expanding daily in a multitude of new

public roles. As educator, legislator, scientist, policeperson, journalist, health administrator, or television personality, she can carry to whatever work she practices an understanding of the need to destroy the old patterns of the macho male and the dependent female. She will realize that rape is not an isolated problem but the result of compounded errors in attitudes that are bases for many other injustices. She will know that this one dramatic crime is only part of a large, intricate web of social patterns, and that the ways of working against it are many and subtle.

Whatever her place in society she will be politically alert and supportive of all legislation that helps women to be honest with themselves and managers of their own destinies. She will know that any law that exploits the vulnerable and the poor is ultimately an arrow in her own side. She will work to change the male chauvinist technique of stereotyping women, and she will also work to educate her sisters to the *responsibilities* of the new equalities that are at hand.

In her private life, as mother, sister, wife, lover, and friend, she will work to fend off the old hatreds and lay grounds for new understanding. This will not be easy. But she might begin by refusing the old put-downs and by resisting the facile solutions in which she has so often abdicated her responsibilities to men. She might make her decisions, particularly in regard to sex, *stick*, instead of vacillating and letting a man make up her mind for her. She will recognize that teasing is childish, a pathetic show of sexual immaturity, and will protect herself with courage, humor, and firmness. Resolute in her determination not to be exploited sexually or psychologically by men, she in turn will refrain from exploiting them financially or for status or other advantages.

She will work to defeat the easy, old stereotypes by being true to herself. Recognizing that attitudes toward women are largely formulated in the family, through example and discussions, she will try to give her sons and daughters a chance to mature free of the binding old sex roles. She will educate those around her to the fact that sex is not "a man's right" but "an important human concern" and work to free her own psyche and those of her children from the pruderies and fears of other centuries, other places. She will realize that it is as hard for the men to break out of their old stereotypes as it is for women, and she will give them understanding and support as they learn to change their attitudes. Vengefulness and hostility are worse than useless; they are self-perpetuating.

If ever it befalls her to become a victim of rape she will have the courage to prosecute, knowing that this is a brave and sisterly act. It is a modern heroine who, in order to save another woman from the trauma she has suffered, takes the stand and faces a defense attorney whose professional advancement depends on destroying her story.

American women often complain that their men are either fascistic or cowardly in their relations with them. Both extremes are manifestations of the failings of the present pattern. The existing roles, built on old dovetailing neuroses, have got to be dismantled. Centuries of warped thinking, canonized by a now perilously creaky legal system, have got to be set aright. The idea that the law is "a net to catch certain kinds of fish" has got to be repaired, if the law is to keep the people's respect.

There is work to be done, work for everyone. Rape-crisis centers have the herculean task of helping victims and sensitizing their communities to the problems of rape. Most police systems need to rethink their attitudes and procedures, and medical services for victims must be improved. Mental health counselors must be oriented to the special traumas of rape victims, especially the very young. Legislators have important laws to rewrite and push through; community action groups and individual citizens must write their elected representatives to impress upon them that new legislation is necessary. Penal procedures are in urgent need of revision, and the press should take a long look at some of the tasteless, dated devices it is still using, even when it knows better. In the courts, attitudes must be upgraded among root-bound judges, lawyers nervous about their win-lose records, and jurors self-righteously aloof from the crimes that are proof of failures in which they share.

There is much soul-searching to be done by everyone connected with television and films, and it would be well if, behind each soul that was searched, there were a woman with a clear idea of what to look for.

There is much work to be done for the new millenium ahead in the realm of human relations. For women, the discovery of their real selves will be an event equaling in the magnitude of its possibilities that of the New World. Or perhaps a more apt metaphor would be that of the reemergence of the lost continent of Atlantis. For they have known all along that it was there.

The world has waited many centuries for science to give women the freedom to be human beings first and women second. No longer need society be divided and crippled by a secret war between the sexes in mutually flagellating roles. Without the festering claims of the old myths, the Bait and the Trap will no longer exist.

Epilogue

After a rape, what happens to the victim? to the offender?

Many of the men in the events cited here were never caught and went on to rape again. Some, although apprehended, wiggled through the loopholes of the legal system but may have been sufficiently shaken by the experience to be deterred from continuing. Others, driven by needs they cannot control, are still compulsively terrorizing women. They will continue to do so until the justice and penal systems are perfected so that these men are not returned to the community unrehabilitated.

The outcome of these cases, necessarily incomplete, is as follows:

— The Jewish divorcee (page 11), after struggling with her feelings about the young Puerto Rican, called her rabbi and discussed the case with him. He advised her to report, which she did, and the young man was arrested.

— The man who raped the girl while on the way to the movies (page 17) had a good alibi, but when caught, confessed and was sentenced to twelve years in prison.

— The flagpole sitter who raped his visiting admirer (page 16) was prosecuted for statutory rape because the victim was under age.

— The garbage man who raped the nine Main Line matrons (page 9) was caught when he attacked a girl of twelve near a school. From his interviews with the man Amir took this last event as a sign of the man's deterioration; he was becoming obsessed with sex and needed ever more helpless victims.

— The man who raped the same woman on three different occasions in her own home and before leaving helped her repair the faulty screen through which he had entered (page 42) was never caught.

— The Vietnam veteran, John, who picked up Jane and her two friends, was caught and charged with fifteen counts of rape, sodomy, oral sex, kidnapping, and assault with a deadly weapon but was sentenced for only four of these; the charge of rape against the second girl, somehow, was among those dropped. (pages 100 and 101)

——The man who assaulted the San Francisco widow on the construction site (page 19) was caught. He had thought himself safe because he knew her English was poor and he counted on her immigrant shyness to inhibit her reporting. But he miscalculated the courage of an old woman whose costly false-teeth plates had been broken.

——The young woman who was raped by the doctor's son after an evening of bridge (page 37) later told her college classmate about the event. The classmate chose not to believe the story about her boyfriend and married him anyhow.

——The man who raped two women in a coffee shop restroom under threat of cutting their bellies with a penknife (page 42) was never caught.

——The man with a stocking over his face who raped two of four women in a grocery store holdup (page 15) was caught. He confessed he did not know why he had done it; the crime had not been part of his plan. Before leaving the scene he managed to get the cash register open and take the $36 within. He then returned the $1 and $2 to the women from whom he had taken the money, but not the $6. In a farewell salute he then gave three clicks of his gun to show that it had not been loaded.

——The man who seized seventeen victims getting off the San Francisco bus in Marin County (page 15) was finally apprehended when he attacked a woman who got away and who immediately went to the police. She returned with them to the scene of the attempted crime and found the man still there, waiting for another victim.

——The book editor who was pair-raped by a former lover and his buddy, unable to have her case prosecuted by the local district attorney's office, at last reports was moving to charge the offenders in a civil case. If the offender is salaried, this can be a worthwhile procedure, for the victim can not only demand reparation for her ordeal, but she can recover court costs. This kind of direct restitution to the victim in some ways makes more sense than the state's prosecution, in which the offender, if convicted, is incarcerated, but the victim receives nothing for what she has suffered.

——The young man with the frightful modus operandi of trying to incinerate his victims never went to trial but was diagnosed as a paranoid schizophrenic and committed to a California state psychiatric hospital with the request that if he were ever to be released, the police were to be notified. Two months later he was diagnosed as cured and released without the police being informed. Within twenty-four hours he tied up a woman, raped her, then set fire to the bed. It was the activation of an automatic sprinkling system by the flames that saved the woman's life, but she was in the hospital for many weeks.

—Dirty Charley was finally caught in a parking lot next to a department store in Oakland when the woman he seized and pulled to the ground quick-wittedly suggested going inside her car. He let her up; before he could stop her, she got into the car and locked it. Furious, he banged on the window, trying to get in at her. This attracted attention and he was arrested.

—The music teacher who was raped by her new pupil did not want to have the offender put in jail, but she wanted him to be deterred from continuing, and if possible to get psychiatric help. She reported it to the police of her small town, whose technique in dealing with such offenders is refined but efficacious. For several weeks the man is called and visited, at home and at work, day and night, by police officers who warn him that the case has been reported, that it may or may not be prosecuted, and that they are watching him. A man who is not really sick or compulsive, just an unfeeling bastard inclined to indulge his supermacho whims, responds very well to such pressures.

Women's groups as well as police are developing creative techniques for dealing with offenders in their communities. In Santa Rosa a man who had a long record of picking up women and children and molesting them was officially admonished and obliged to wear on his car at all times a sign saying "Do not accept a ride from this man."

—Among the many cases of the known offender that never reached the police was that of the young Honolulu woman who became pregnant on a blind date. She never saw the man again, and soon afterward left the Islands. Her tragedy went even deeper than what had been one night of a forgettable celebration for the navy lieutenant: the same thing had happened to her once before. The fact that she had already been through a similar pregnancy terminated by a messy abortion did not seem to increase her strength to resist. On the contrary, she seemed more than ever forlornly vulnerable.

How much psychological damage does rape do to a victim? The reaction may take place soon afterwards and be violent, like that of a seventy-five-year-old Baltimore woman who threw herself out of a window to her death after being raped and robbed of $1.39 on her way to church.

Or it may take a hundred subtler forms, hurtful both to the woman and to those around her: trust replaced by suspicion, a once free and optimistic spirit replaced by withdrawal, anxiety, and hostility. Years later, other men who will never understand why may become victims of her ill will, as the battle between men and women is perpetuated.

Listen to Jane, two years after her experience with the Vietnam veteran: "I've become a watcher; now I'm always watching. I don't trust people. I'm always testing them. I still dream of revenge, of stabbing someone like John over and over. I'm really angry with men. They don't understand women, don't want to."

And what of the very young victims? Listen to Linda: "It wasn't even a real rape, when I was twelve, on a beach in Mexico. I got away. But for years afterwards I didn't want to go back to that beach; I didn't even want to go to that country."

The Berkeley coed who was crossing campus to turn in her English paper, although seemingly compliant, was in fact deeply wounded by her experience. In addition to the usual shock of the victim she received another, because she was one of the gentle, trusting "flower children," and her offender was black. She wanted to believe that black men were her brothers. The brave girl's faith in the essential goodness of people was shaken, and trust, already in short supply in a cynical society, received one more setback. She reported the case but refused to prosecute.

INDEX